*For lovers of fashion and fabric who want to make
something with a touch of 'Je ne sais quoi'.
We salute you.*

Sewing Your Perfect
CAPSULE WARDROBE

*5 key pieces with full-size patterns
that can be tailored to your style*

Arianna Cadwallader & Cathy McKinnon

Photography Amanda Thomas

KYLE BOOKS

CONTENTS

PREPARATION AND TECHNIQUE

Fitting

Fabric

Finish

THE CAPSULE COLLECTION

Arianna and Cathy

HELLO,

we're Arianna and Cathy, designers and devotees to making clothes. We've written this book to show you how to create your own capsule wardrobe. The beauty of a capsule wardrobe is that it doesn't chase the trends. It's essentially a collection of perfectly fitted pieces that act as a foundation to the rest of your garments. The capsule concept was introduced in the 1970s by Susie Faux, owner of the London boutique 'Wardrobe'. The idea was reinvented by Donna Karan when she launched her own capsule wardrobe of seven interchangeable work-wear pieces in the mid-1980s.

Since then, the concept has become a lifestyle choice for many women. Having a more minimal wardrobe can give you a sense of freedom. Freedom from the anxiety of too much choice, from the pressure to follow the latest fast fashion, and freedom to choose your own style. Imagine opening your wardrobe and seeing a classic collection of clothes, beautifully pressed and ready to wear, made by you. Clothes that last season to season. Clothes that owe their life to your creativity. Their fabric, cut, colour and detailed finish, all born out of your desire to create something new and unique. This is the capsule wardrobe.

So, where do you start?

Well, we've done the hard work for you. We've taken inspiration from couture and high-street fashion, researched trends, studied the history of pattern shaping and designed key items that will serve as a foundation to your wardrobe. You just need to decide which patterns you want to make and which clothes you want to pair them with from your existing wardrobe.

Making your own capsule wardrobe doesn't mean throwing out all your old clothes and only allowing minimal pieces to grace your hangers. It's about streamlining what you already have and pairing them with key pieces you'll make in this book. That way you'll have a collection you'll actually love to wear. The foundation to any capsule wardrobe are the key pieces. Get these items right and you'll have a mix and match collection that will last (almost) a lifetime.

Arianna & Cathy X

The beauty of a **capsule wardrobe** *is that it doesn't chase the trends.*

Introducing the five key pieces

Each key piece in this book has a main pattern and a sister pattern - a more relaxed and informal take on the original pattern which means you have the choice to go either smart, relaxed, or both.

①

THE VEST TOP

Go skinny
This vest is ideal for everyday wear. This pattern has a lovely racer back detail.

Go loose
The sister version is more open with a wider arched hem and a skinnier back.

②

THE SKIRT

Go fitted
This skirt follows a midi line that skims below the knee and sits on the hips.

Go flared
The more informal sister version is a charming a-line mini.

3

THE SHIFT DRESS

Go simple
This dress is a semi-fitted shift which sits just above the knee.

Go informal
This shift dress is an over-sized 'tent' style which drapes beautifully.

4

THE TROUSERS

Go straight
A textbook classic straight leg trouser with a mid rise waist.

Go wide
The sister version has a wider leg for a more casual, relaxed vibe.

5

THE BLOUSE

Go relaxed
This blouse is gently fitted with full length sleeves and a mandarin collar.

Go slouchy
This everyday blouse has a low v neck and a cute elastic cuff.

FITTING

Taking measurements

The three golden measurements in dressmaking are the bust, waist and hip. They underpin the structure of every pattern and it's worth updating these measurements yearly as they have a tendency to change.

Few of us are standard high-street sizes, so it's really important to get your measurements spot on before you go near a pair of scissors. Dressmaking preparation is all about measurements. They're the building blocks to all garment construction and, although it takes

a bit of time to take your own measurements, it's definitely worth it. Get a friend to help as the measurement will alter each time you bend or stretch. All you need is a tape measure, a length of ribbon or string, a pencil and a sheet of paper.

The list over the page is more comprehensive and many of the measurements are essential only when drafting your own patterns. It's not necessary to take all these measurements to make each of the garments in this book, but they'll be handy for future dressmaking and they can help when adjusting a pattern too.

METRIC/IMPERIAL CONVERSION CHART

1mm – $^1/_{32}$"	3cm – $1^1/_4$"	12cm – $4^3/_4$"	45cm – $17^1/_2$"
2mm – $^1/_{16}$"	3.5cm – $1^3/_8$"	13cm – $5^1/_4$"	50cm – $19^3/_4$"
3mm – $^1/_8$"	4cm – $1^1/_2$"	14cm – $5^1/_2$"	60cm – $23^1/_2$"
5mm – $^3/_{16}$"	5cm – 2"	15cm – 6"	67.5cm – $26^1/_2$"
6mm – $^1/_4$"	6cm – $2^3/_8$"	20cm – 8"	80cm – $31^1/_2$"
1cm – $^3/_8$"	6.5cm – $2^1/_2$"	21.25cm – $8^1/_4$"	92cm – $36^1/_4$"
1.25cm – $^1/_2$"	7cm – $2^3/_4$"	22.5cm – $8^1/_2$"	98cm – $38^1/_2$"
1.5cm – $^5/_8$"	7.5cm – 3"	25cm – 10"	115cm – $45^1/_4$"
2cm – $^3/_4$"	10cm – 4"	30cm – $11^3/_4$"	127.5cm – $50^1/_4$"
2.5cm – 1"	11cm – $4^1/_4$"	40cm – $15^3/_4$"	140cm – 55"

TOP TIPS FOR MEASURING

◈ Always begin measuring with the start of the tape measure, working from zero.

◈ Don't change from metric to imperial, or vice versa. Stick with one system throughout.

- - - - - - - - - - - - -

How to get perfect measurements

1 Be aware of what clothing you have on when taking your measurements. It's best to wear your usual underwear.

2 Stand in a natural posture, but without any footwear.

3 Tie a length of ribbon or string around your waist. Your waist is where you have a natural indentation if you lean over to one side. This may not be where you want your garment to sit, but you can use the ribbon as a reference point when measuring, as many measurements start and end at this point.

4 Using your tape measure, take each measurement on the chart opposite Keep the tape measure flat and level. There should be no excess room between you and it but the tape measure should be comfy, not tight. Fill in each measurement as you go.

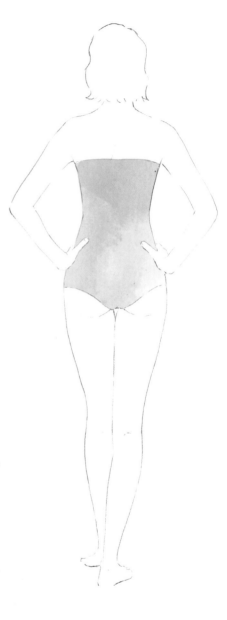

PATTERN KNOWHOW

Make a toile for every garment as your measurements will need fine-tuning once you have adjusted the flat pattern (see page 18).

- - - - - - - - - - - - -

MEASUREMENT CHART

	YOUR MEASUREMENT

TORSO

BUST (A) Around the fullest part of your bust.

WAIST (B) Around your waist where the ribbon is tied

HIPS (C) Around the fullest part of your bottom and hips, approximately 18–23cm/ 7–9 inches depending on your shape

UPPER HIP Around your hips, on your top hip bone, approximately 7.5cm/3 inches below the ribbon

WAIST TO HIP From waist to hip line

OVER BUST Around the top of your bust with the tape nestled under your armpit

UNDER BUST Around your bust where the bra line usually sits

POINT TO POINT Nipple to nipple

ACROSS FRONT Across your front, mid-armhole to mid-armhole

ACROSS BACK Across your back, mid-armhole to mid-armhole

SHOULDER LINE From the side of your neck to your shoulder point (a dimple appears when raising your arm to the side)

SHOULDER LINE TO BUST POINT From the point nearest your neck to your bust point

SHOULDER LINE TO WAIST From the point nearest your neck to your waist

NECKLINE

YOUR MEASUREMENT

The neck hollow is the deepest point between your collarbone. Use it as your natural neckline. The nape is at the base of the back of the neck where it feels a little bony.

NECK HOLLOW TO BUST POINT
Straight down from your neck hollow to your bust point

NECK HOLLOW TO WAIST
Straight down from your neck hollow to your waist

NECK HOLLOW TO FLOOR
Straight down your front from your neck hollow to the floor

NAPE TO WAIST From the centre back of your nape straight down to the centre of your back

* NAPE TO GROUND From the centre back of your nape straight down to the floor

* Handy to have a buddy to help

ARMS

SHOULDER TO ELBOW

From your shoulder point (the dimple if you raise your arm) to your elbow, with your elbow bent at a right angle

TOP OF SHOULDER TO WRIST

From your shoulder point to your wrist, with your arm in neutral position (with a natural kink)

INSIDE ARM TO WRIST

From your armpit to your wrist, with your arm in neutral position (with a natural kink)

ARM AROUND TOP

The circumference of your upper arm, with your elbow bent

ELBOW

The circumference of your elbow, with your elbow bent

FOREARM

The circumference of your forearm

WRIST

The circumference of your wrist

ARMHOLE

From your shoulder point, under your armpit and back to your shoulder point

LEGS

**YOUR
MEASUREMENT**

* INSIDE LEG SEAM

From the top of your inside leg to the floor

* OUTSIDE LEG

From your waist to the floor

INSIDE LEG TO KNEE

From the top of your inside leg to your knee

THIGH

The circumference of the fullest part of your thigh – also note how far that line is from your waist and from the top of the inside leg seam

CALF

The circumference of the fullest part of your calf – also make a note of how far that line is from the top of the inside leg seam

ANKLE

The circumference of your ankle

RISE

Sitting on a firm chair, from your waist to where your bottom and the chair meet

CROTCH

Down from your front waist, between your legs, and up to your back waist

* Handy to have a buddy to help

Understanding patterns and symbols

Pattern symbols for dressmaking are pretty much universal. Whether you are using patterns from this book, a bought pattern or creating your own, the following symbols and terms will become very familiar to you.

Stars

These stars need to be transferred onto the fabric in order to line up your pattern pieces correctly. They can be transferred using either tailor's tacks, carbon copying or pin marking.

Place on fold

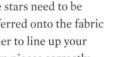

This symbol shows where you need to line up the pattern with a fold along the fabric. Some pattern pieces are given as half pieces because the other half is symmetrical. Fold the fabric and align the 'place on fold' mark on the pattern along the fabric fold. Once you cut around the cutting line you will have a complete piece.

Grainline

The grainline is parallel to the selvedge edge (tightly woven edges) of the fabric. If you align the grainline marking so that it runs parallel to the selvedge, your finished garment will drape correctly.

Notches and snips

Notches and snips are used to match different pieces of a pattern together. Notches are small single triangles and snips are overlaid double triangles. For the notches, cut a small triangle, making sure you don't cut into the seam allowance. For snips simply cut a single 'snip' line.

Buttonhole

This shows you where to make a buttonhole. Transfer the marks using tailor's tacks or pins (see page 26). After completing the buttonholes, lay that part of the garment onto the part that needs the buttons. Use the buttonholes to mark the positions for the buttons.

Gathering

These symbols are stars with arrows at the beginning and end of a line of gathering. You'll find them on sleeve pattern pieces, for example. Transfer the marks using tailor's tacks or pins (see page 26). To gather, sew two parallel lines of tacking (basting) stitch between the stars and within the seam allowance, then gently and evenly gather up the fabric to match the corresponding parts of the garment.

Pleats

Pleat markings are shown as two parallel lines with an arrow in the direction the pleat should go. Transfer the marks using tailor's tacks or pins (see page 26).

Lengthening and shortening lines

These parallel lines indicate the best place to adjust the pattern when either lengthening or shortening a garment. (See instructions for lengthening and shortening patterns on page 19.)

Pattern sizing and grading

The patterns in this book come in six sizes, numbered 1–6. Once you have completed your measurements, you can see which size of pattern you fit most closely. Remember, we don't all fit into universal sizes. You might be a size 4 around the bust, but a size 6 across the waist and hips. If necessary, you can grade the pattern pieces to fit your measurements perfectly.

Grading is the skill of changing a pattern to fit your own exact measurements. So it's very important to get your measurements correct right from the start. For example, if your waist is size 2 and your lower hips are size 4, you'll need to adapt the pattern pieces for the skirt so that the garment will fit you.

How to grade a pattern

1 Working with the pattern for size 2 and using a ruler, mark your measurement for waist to fullest hips on the front and back pattern pieces. Then mark your actual hip measurement on both pattern pieces, including extra for ease.

2 Now redraw a freehand line on the pattern from the existing waist to the new hip width. Keeping the shape smooth, continue down to the hemline, parallel to the existing lines on the pattern. This will be your new pattern shape.

Ease

This is the clever part of dressmaking that enables our clothes to skim and drape the way we want them to – and it's important. If we didn't incorporate ease we wouldn't be able to walk or bend our arms or sit down! All patterns include ease to different extents depending on the type of garment and style, so be sure to include the correct amount of ease if you are altering a pattern. You'll find the ease measurement at the start of each project.

EASE GUIDELINES

SEMI FITTED	
BUST	Add 7–10cm
WAIST	Add 5–7cm
HIPS	Add 5–7cm
RELAXED FIT	
BUST	Add 10–15cm
WAIST	Add 7–10cm
HIPS	Add 7–10cm
LOOSE FIT	
BUST	Add 15–20cm
WAIST	Add 10–13cm
HIPS	Add 10–13cm

Transferring notches and other markings

You need to mark notches and other markings onto the corresponding fabric pieces to help you join the pieces together correctly.

Transferring notches

Mark notches by cutting small triangular shapes into the seam allowance. Make them about 5mm deep, so they do not extend beyond the seam allowance.

Using tailor's tacks

Attach the pattern piece to the fabric. Using a contrasting colour of thread, make two or three big loopy stitches through the centre of the star, the paper and all the layers of fabric. Gently remove the paper pattern, then carefully separate the two layers of fabric but, as you do, snip each tailor's tack to leave a tiny tuft of coloured thread in both pieces of fabric.

Pin marking

Insert a pin through the centre of each star on the pattern and the fabric pieces. Gently remove the paper, leaving the pins in place. Mark the position of the pinhead with chalk or a fabric marker on the wrong side of the top piece of fabric and mark the other end of the pin on the wrong side of the bottom piece of fabric.

Carbon copying

Mainly used for marking darts and pleats. Place two layers of carbon paper, carbon to fabric, between the two fabric pieces, wrong sides together. Place the paper pattern on the fabric. Use a tracing wheel and ruler to mark the dart. This will transfer the markings onto the wrong side of both pieces of fabric.

Tracing off patterns

Once you have graded the original pattern to make a new pattern to fit your shape, or if you are using the original as supplied in this book, we recommend tracing it off so that you can adapt and change it as much as you want without spoiling the original. Then you can trace the original as many times as you like to make various adaptations of the garments.

You can use any kind of paper to lay over the pattern as long as you can see through it – baking parchment, tracing paper or pattern paper are all useful.

1 Lay your paper over the original pattern and carefully trace the outlines with a sharp pencil. Make sure you transfer all the markings.

2 If you plan to incorporate design alterations such as necklines and sleeve length or sizing changes, you'll need to do this before you cut around each pattern piece.

3 Make sure you have incorporated seam allowances of 1.5cm if necessary on your new pattern (seam allowance is included in the pattern pieces). Transfer all notches and other markings to your new pattern and cut it out.

4 Make a note on the pattern about the new design for your own records. Add the date and draw a little image of the garment so you can always identify it easily.

5 You are now ready to cut out the fabric for your garment or for a toile.

Cutting out the fabric

Before you cut out the fabric, you must wash and iron it to remove any excess dye and to allow for any shrinkage so that the garment will keep its shape once made. Each type of fabric has its own washing settings, so seek advice from the fabric shop as to what's best.

1 Refer to the suggested fabric layout for your pattern to see the best way to place the pattern pieces. Fold the fabric as recommended.

2 Lay the pattern pieces flat on the fabric, following the layout, especially in relation to grainlines and foldlines.

3 Using the type of pins that work best with your fabric (see page 26), pin the pattern pieces onto the fabric. Use enough pins to keep the pattern pieces flat but don't overpin as this can cause the fabric to ruck up. If you are using a fabric, such as silk or leather, that 'bruises' easily from pin punctures, use soft weights instead. You can make your own soft weights, similar to bean bags, to any size.

4 Using fabric shears, cut around the outside of the pattern pieces, close to the cutting line.

5 Transfer all the markings, notches and stars onto the fabric (see page 17).

6 Remove the pins and carefully peel the pattern pieces off the fabric and place to one side. You are now ready to sew your garment together.

MAKING A TOILE

A toile is a test version of a garment but made from cheaper fabric. It can also be called a muslin. It's a good idea to use a cheap fabric, but it should have a similar weight and drape to the fabric for the finished garment.

Toiles are a valuable investment because these initial mock-ups help you to make sure all the measurements are correct before cutting into expensive fabric for the finished garment. No matter how accurate flat pattern pieces are, they only really come to life when they take shape in three-dimensional form.

Making a toile allows you to see what the pattern really looks like and to make additional tweaks, cuts and alterations. We recommend making a minimum of one toile per garment. Sometimes you may want to make more, especially if you are tackling an intricate garment such as a pair of tailored trousers.

Lengthening and shortening patterns

You may find that your measurements are longer or shorter than the pattern. You may be shorter in the body or have long arms or legs, for example. Lengthening and shortening patterns is a great skill – you can alter any pattern and remodel it for your own body shape

Shortening

1 Using the markings on the pattern, fold the pattern underneath itself to match the chosen shorter length.

2 Either pin this fold or use sticky tape to keep it in place.

3 Redraw the cutting line, if necessary, to give a smooth seamline.

Lengthening

1 Place a piece of paper underneath the pattern and cut along the parallel lines and extend the pattern to match the desired length. The paper underneath will act as your extension.

2 Pin or use sticky tape to attach the pattern to the extra paper.

3 Redraw the cutting line for a smooth seamline.

PATTERN KNOWHOW

The best places to change length are where the shape of the pattern doesn't change dramatically. Look for the parallel lines that indicate the best place to lengthen or shorten any given pattern piece.

Darts

Darts are folds sewn into the fabric to manage fullness so that garments fit around a body's curves. Single-pointed and double-pointed darts reduce ease and enhance the fit of your garments. We explain below how to sew existing single-pointed darts for the bust and how to add new double-pointed darts.

Sewing single-pointed darts

Single-pointed darts take fullness out from a seam and are often used to give a closer fit around the bust. Bust darts will stop a garment riding up at the front on women with fuller busts. Single-pointed darts are also used at the waist if there is a waist seam, for example.

1 Working on the fabric, pinch the right sides of the dart together at the seam, matching up your tailor tacks or markings. Hold the dart so that the rest of the fabric falls away, making it easier to work with. **(A)**

2 Secure the fold with pins at both ends. Using a ruler, draw a straight guideline for the dart from the cutting line to the dart point with chalk. **(B)**

3 Using straight stitch, sew the dart from the cutting line, along your guideline, to the point of the dart. Sew off the fabric. **(C)**

4 Cut the excess threads long so that you can tie them into a knot. This secures the stitching and gives you a nice sharp point.

5 Press your stitch line, then press the folded fabric in the dart down towards the hem.

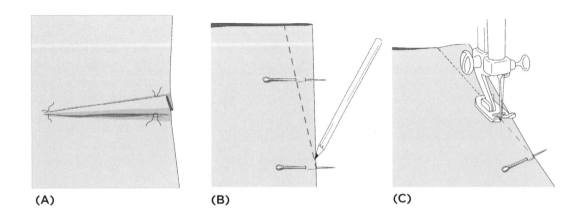

(A)   (B)   (C)

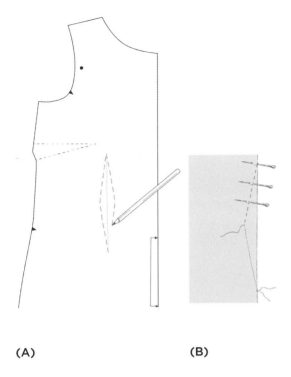

(A)   **(B)**

Adding double-pointed darts

It you want to make a garment more fitted around the middle of the body, these darts work wonders. They can be used to create a more tailored shape on the front and/or back of a garment. They can be quite tricky to position correctly, so it helps to work with a toile and have a fitting buddy.

1 Try on your toile. Pinch the fabric on each side of the centre line where you want to the garment to be more fitted. Place a pin to secure the widest point of each pinch.

2 You'll see that the pinch of fabric naturally fades away above and below the pin. Mark the top and bottom ends of each pinch with a pin.

3 Take the toile off, with the pins still in place. Lay the garment out so that one dart is flat.

4 Measure down from the underarm, along the side seam. Note the measurements to the level of the widest part of the dart. Repeat for the other dart. If the measurements to the widest point of each dart are different, take the average measurement and use that for both darts.

5 Repeat steps 4–5 to establish the position of top and bottom ends of both darts.

6 Now measure the widest part of each dart. If they differ, use the average measurement. Multiply this by two to give the total dart width.

7 In a similar way, also check that all points on both darts are the same distance from the centre line.

8 Once you have all the measurements and feel happy about transferring them to the wrong side of the toile, take all the pins out. Turn the toile inside out.

9 Transfer all your markings onto the wrong side of the toile, flip the fabric to the right side and simply mirror the marks you have made. Check all the measurements to make sure the positioning is correct.

10 Using a ruler, draw two lines to join both ends of the widest point to the top point of each dart. Repeat for the bottom point. This will give you two long diamond shapes. **(A)**

11 Pinch and pin the diamond shape in the same way as a single pointed dart. Pin, then sew along the diagonal lines to secure the darts **(B)**. Start in the middle of the dart and sew down to bottom point. Sew off the fabric. Flip the fabric round and sew from the middle of the dart until the top point. You can reverse stitch in the middle to secure the stitching in place. The dart needs to be nice and smooth following the natural contours of the body.

12 When you are happy with the dart placements, do the toile, then transfer these on to your paper pattern. Mark the top, bottom and widest points onto your pattern pieces to make a diamond shape.

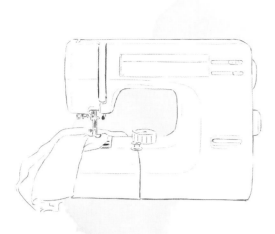

Making a full bust adjustment

Sewing patterns are drafted for a B cup so if you are larger than that, as well as being too tight around the bust, you may notice your garment will be too short at the waist or ride up in the middle. A full bust adjustment will add fullness to a garment around the bust area without losing the fit at the waist and the shoulders.

When incorporating a full bust adjustment work with the size that matches your over bust measurement (see page 13), not your full bust as the pattern maybe too big across the back, shoulders and armholes.

1 Find how much adjustment you need to make. Subtract the over-bust measurement from the bust measurement. Then divide the result by two. For example, 98cm (bust) – 92cm (over-bust) = 6cm; 6cm ÷ 2 = 3cm. Then divide that total by two, so the bust adjustment can be incorporated in both front pieces.

2 Trace off the front bodice pattern, to the waistline, from the original pattern onto a larger sheet of paper. Transfer the original dart markings. Cut the pattern out.

3 Hold the new paper pattern to your chest and mark your bust point. Mark this point with an 'X'. Now move this point 2.5cm closer to the side seam to avoid Madonna style tip.

4 Lay the pattern flat and measure 2.5cm

from your bust point along the centre line of the original dart. Mark this as the point of the new dart. Draw a line along the centre of the dart at the side seam to the new point. Cut along this line.

5 Draw a line straight down from the X to the waistline, parallel to the centre front line.

6 Draw another line from the X to the first notch in the armhole (roughly a third of the way along the armhole from the side seam). **(A)**

7 Cut along the line from the waistline to the X, then continue to within 1–2mm from the armhole notch. The pattern should hinge and move easily at that point.

8 Draw a third line, 5cm up from, and parallel to, the waistline.

9 Place the pattern onto a new piece of paper and secure it with sticky tape along the centre front, neckline and shoulder edges.

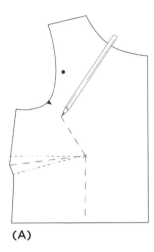

(A)

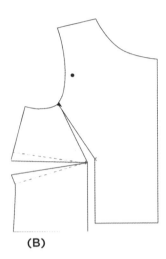

(B)

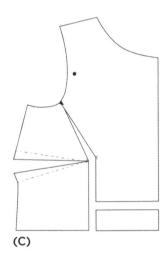

(C)

10 Open up the cut from the waistline to the armhole notch by 1–2cm **(B)**. Secure in place.

11 Open up the dart cut in order to add your full bust adjustment, 1.25cm in our example. Secure in place.

12 You'll notice that the waistline has dropped on the dart side. Cut along the line parallel to the waistline, just from the centre front to the previous cut. Move the piece you have cut off so that the bottom edge follows the original waistline **(C)**. Secure in place.

13 Redraw the lines that need reshaping, including the adjusted dart.

14 Once you have completed the bust adjustment, make a toile to check the fit and adjust before using your chosen fabric.

Attaching to a garment

To reattach the bodice to the main garment pattern, line up the centre front line. The bodice piece will be sticking out to the side, so simply redraw in a new curve for the original lower dart line to meet your hip line. This new line will be a soft curve to realign with your garment.

Making a small bust adjustment

If your bust measurement is less than 5cm more than your over-bust measurement, you'll need to make a small bust adjustment.

1 Find how much adjustment you need to make. Hold the front pattern piece up to your chest and make a note of how much the centre front of the pattern overlaps the mid-point on your chest. This is your reduction measurement.

2 Repeat steps 2–13 opposite for making a full-bust adjustment, but overlap the pattern sections on the side seam by using your reduction measurement and also on the waist. Again, make a toile to check and adjust the fit.

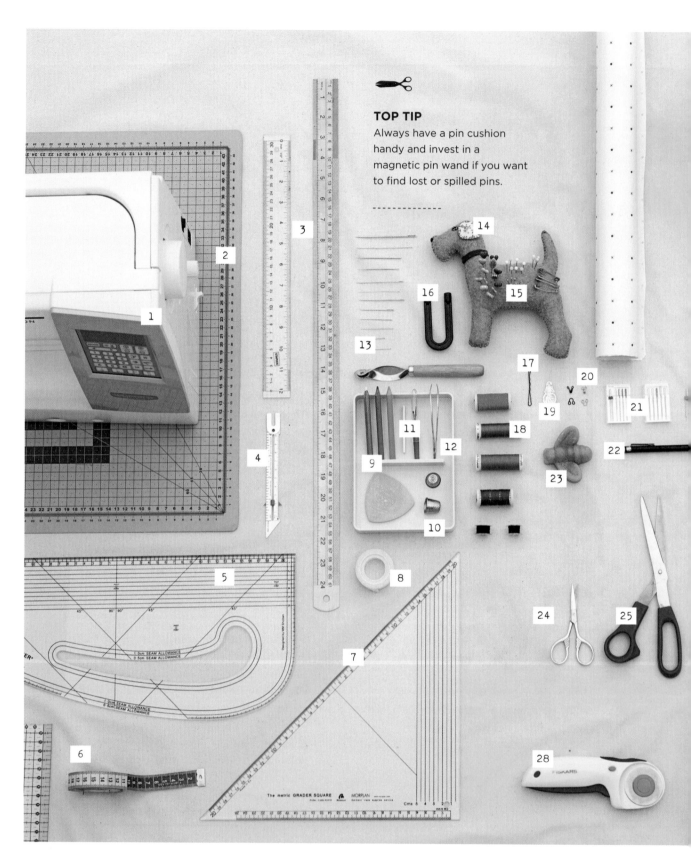

TOP TIP

Always have a pin cushion handy and invest in a magnetic pin wand if you want to find lost or spilled pins.

Your sewing kit

It's important to have a few decent sewing tools to start with and your kit will expand over time. There are some brilliant tools to help the ever-improving sewer.

1 Sewing machine, well-maintained **2** Cutting mat
3 Rulers, a clear plastic one and a more heavy-duty metal one
4 Measuring gauge, which can be handmade
5 Pattern master, for the more advanced **6** Tape measure
7 Set square **8** Sticky tape **9** Fabric markers, such as tailors' chalk in block or pencil form, air/water erasable pen, or carbon paper and tracing wheel **10** Thimble **11** Seam ripper (quick unpick) **12** Tweezers **13** Hand sewing needles **14** Pin cushion, bought or homemade; one to attach to your wrist is handy
15 Pins **16** Magnet, to pick up the pins! **17** Kirby grip for sewing buttons **18** Assortment of thread **19** Quick threader
20 Hooks and eyes **21** Machine needles including twin needles
22 Pencil **23** Beeswax, to keep thread smooth
24 Small scissors for snipping threads **25** Paper scissors
26 Pinking shears **27** Sewing shears, sharp and good quality
28 Rotary cutter **29** Fabric weight **30** Assortment of buttons
31 Point turner **32** Dressmaker's ham, a cushion for curved pressing to allow for a better garment fit **33** Iron
34 Ironing board and sleeve ironing board **35** Loop turner

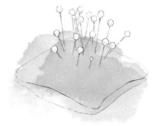

PINS AND NEEDLES

Even though they are the smallest tool in the sewing kit, they play a crucial part in dressmaking. They hold fabric pieces together, secure darts and seams, allow you to ease sleeves into armholes and help you make the tweaks required to get the final fit just so.

PINS

Dressmaking pins come in a range of different thicknesses, lengths and types of point, and we recommend buying various types to cover all bases. A pin should glide into fabric without causing any unnecessary drag.

Dressmaker: A stainless-steel, medium-length pin that's suitable for most clothing projects. Choose pins for medium- to heavyweight fabrics and extra-sharp for lightweight fabrics.

Pleating: These extra-fine, shorter pins are suitable for the most delicate of fabrics.

Plastic-headed: Available in all different shapes, sizes and colours. Be careful when using these as the heads can melt under a hot iron.

Entomology: Originally used to pin insects, these long, fine pins are good to work with on delicate silks and antique fabrics.

Glass-headed: With small, ball-shaped heads, these pins are easy to find and handle. Plus, they're heat resistant

Dipped-head: Also called Applique, these small painted pins can be quickly and accurately placed.

Ballpoint: These are only for knits, as they don't pierce the yarn, but slip between the knitted loops instead.

Pins with a small metal head are useful when a garment requires frequent pressing as the hot iron won't melt the pinhead. They're also good for marking notches and stars.

Pins with wide-plastic heads are handy as they lay flat if you need to run a tape measure over the top. They're also easy to spot.

HAND SEWING NEEDLES

A high-quality assortment pack will contain a mixture of needles of various lengths and thicknesses.

Sharps: For all-purpose hand sewing and work well for the majority of dressmaking projects.

Easy thread: All-purpose needles for sewers who have difficulty threading other needles

Quilting: These needles are short, with a small eye. Perfect for quick, accurate stitching.

Darner: A long needle with a long eye and a sharp point. Perfect for mending holes.

Leather: A needle with a wedge-shaped point designed to cut leather and other heavy fabrics.

Curved: A cleverly curved needle that's useful for getting into tight corners.

SEWING MACHINE NEEDLES

Invest in a good selection of needles. Sewing machine needles are available in a range of sizes to suit different fabrics. Dress-making needles come in a range of sizes. Regular point needles are for woven fabrics.

Universal: Available in a wide range of sizes, this slightly rounded-point needle can be used on knits, but is also sharp enough for woven fabrics.

Ball-point: A round-tip needle for sewing knits, as the tip doesn't pierce the fabric threads.

Twin point: Made with two needles on a single shaft, this needle creates a parallel row of stitches for a decorative finish and pintucks.

Twin ball-point: These have a rounded point for sweaters and jerseys.

Twin stretch: Similar to the ball-point but with a less rounded point for super stretchy fabrics such as Lycra®.

Wedge point: For sewing leather, faux leather and dress plastic.

Jeans: A strong needle made for sewing multiple layers and tough materials such as denim.

Embroidery: A needle with a groove above the eye designed to sew embroidery without shredding decorative thread.

Needle sizes

European sizing for needles is numbered from 70 to 120. The American sizing system is numbered from 10 to 19. The higher numbers are thicker needles and the lower numbers are finer needles.

10/70: For light fabrics such as silk, taffeta and chiffon.

12/80: For medium-weight fabric such as jersey, linen and cotton.

14/90: For medium- to heavy-weight fabric.

16/100: For heavy fabrics such as denim, canvas and tweed.

18/110: For upholstery fabrics.

19/120: For very heavy upholstery fabrics and thick denim.

Change your needle after completing a couple of garments as a blunt or bent needle can damage fabric and cause skipped stitches.

FABRIC

One of the best things about making your own clothes is having the freedom to bring your own style to a garment. The wrong decision can mean ruining a project and starting all over again. When buying fabric think about the sort of print you like, whether you prefer a vintage fabric, the colour and weight you want.

There is a vast array of fabrics to choose from, and they are all either woven or knitted. Knitted fabrics have more stretch than woven fabrics.

Fabric can be made from plant fibres (cotton or linen), animal fibres (silk or wool) or synthetic fibres (such as polyester or nylon).

Dressmaking fabric usually comes in two widths – 140cm and 115cm. The patterns in this book include layouts for both. We have also given approximate fabric quantities so that you have an idea of how much fabric to buy. You might prefer to buy a bit extra to be on the safe side. It's better to have slightly too much than not enough!

It's best to visit a fabric shop and unroll the fabric to feel the texture and see how it will drape. Do you like the feel? How about the colour? Think about the garment you want to make, when you're likely to wear it and how you want it to handle. The shift dress, for example, will have a very different finish if made in a lightweight printed cotton rather than a heavier wool tweed.

Each fabric will have specific washing and care instructions, so check for these on the label and get advice from the shop if you have any questions.

Once you have purchased your fabric, it will require pre-treatment before you can begin making your garment. This involves washing, drying and ironing the fabric the same way you would if it was the final garment. This will remove any excess dye and allow for shrinkage so that the finished garment keeps its shape.

If your finished wool trousers and silk skirt will take trips to the dry cleaners then you will need to dry clean the fabric first. The same applies if you prefer to handwash silk and wool. You will need to handwash these delicate fabrics first and lay them out flat to dry.

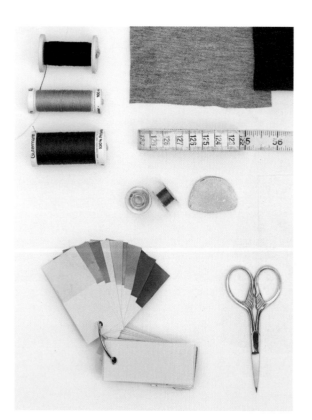

You won't need to wash pleather/faux leather or 100 per cent polyester fabric as they are synthetic. It's always worth asking for advice on how best to care for the fabric when you are purchasing it.

Thread

It's useful to have a basic selection of threads, but you'll always need specific colours to match fabric for your projects.

Choose your thread for projects wisely as it's effectively holding your garment together. There are so many threads on the market in an array of colours and weights, so a useful rule of thumb is to choose a thread that matches your fabric in weight. You wouldn't use a heavy-duty thread with a light cotton fabric.

Polyester thread is an all-purpose thread and is great for dressmaking projects. It has a slight give, which means it's less likely to break. We used dual-purpose polyester thread for all the projects in this book.

Cotton thread can break easily as it has very little stretch, but it's great for hand basting (tacking) and to match with lightweight cotton or delicately woven fabrics, as they don't have much stretch either.

Silk thread is super-fine and has great elasticity and strength. It doesn't leave any holes, making it perfect for delicate fabrics and wool.

Buttonhole thread is a strong, heavier thread and is great for securing buttons and stitching buttonholes by hand.

Buttons

It's handy to have a selection of colours and sizes available although you may need to buy new ones to match specific projects.

FABRIC GUIDE

Acrylic a warm, synthetic wool-like fabric, that can be worn all year. **Best for:** active wear and sports wear

Calico a plain, woven cotton fabric available in different weights. **Best for:** making a toile

Challis a soft, lightweight fabric made of cotton, polyester, or silk/wool blend. It has a good drape and slightly brushed surface. **Best for:** dresses and would work well for the sister dress (see page 110), main blouse (see page 144) and floaty maxi skirt (see page 96).

Chambray a plain, woven cotton fabric made with blue and white threads to look similar to denim. It can be found in lightweights and heavier weights. **Best for:** casual dresses, tops and trousers and would work well for the main shift dress (see page 100), both skirt styles (see page 80), the sister trousers (see page 133), the culottes (see page 142) and the mullet skirt (see page 98).

Cheesecloth a plain-dyed, lightweight, loosely woven cotton fabric with a gauze-like appearance. **Best for:** lightweight dresses, blouses, skirts and trousers and would work well for the sister blouse (see page 157).

Chiffon a sheer, fine woven fabric with a luxurious, floaty and delicate appearance. Silk chiffon is more breathable, whereas polyester chiffon is more durable. **Best for:** slips and blouses, such as the main and sister blouse styles (see pages 144 and 157).

Corduroy a medium-weight cotton fabric with a pile in parallel lines. Although velvety to the touch, it is durable. **Best for:** jackets, shirts and trousers, such as the main trousers (see page 122).

Cotton the most versatile of all fibres, so it's good for inexperienced sewers. It can be knitted or woven into many different guises and the most popular are listed here. These come in different weights from fine lawn to heavy denim.

Best for: Lighter cottons are ideal for womenswear and sleepwear, while the sturdier cotton weaves work best for clothes that need to be durable. The main shift dress (see page 100) was made in cotton chambray. The sister blouse (see page 157) was made using cotton lawn with Swiss knot.

Crepe a soft, lightweight fabric made with a crinkled thread. It's often made from cotton or silk, but can be made from any fibre. It has great drape and is easy to sew. **Best for:** lightweight dresses, blouses, skirts and trousers and would work well with the shift dress (see page 100) and sister dress (see page 110), sister skirt (see page 92), sister wide-leg trousers (see page 133) and culottes (see page 142).

Denim a sturdy, heavyweight cotton fabric synonymous with jeans **Best for:** trousers and jackets and would work well with the main shift dress (see page 100), the straight trousers (see page 122) and the main skirt (see page 80).

Drill usually a heavyweight cotton, this versatile fabric with a twill weave is strong and durable. **Best for:** uniforms and workwear. Would work for the main trousers (see page 122).

Faux leather an imitation with the look and feel of genuine leather. Materials range from plastic to flexible fabrics that are coated and embossed to mimic real leather. A cheaper and more workable alternative to real leather. **Best for:** coats, dresses and skirts and would work well for the main shift dress (see page 100). The main skirt (see page 80) was made from chocolate-coloured faux leather.

Jacquard a dense medium- to heavyweight fabric with an elaborate pattern woven into it. It can be made from cotton, silk or synthetic fibres **Best for:** skirts, jackets and trousers and would work well with the mullet skirt (see page 98) and a more formal interpretation of the main shift dress (see page 100) and cigarette pants (see page 140).

Jersey a knitted fabric that is light, flexible and warm.

It comes in multiple weights and can be made from cotton, wool, silk or manufactured fibres. **Best for:** T-shirts, dresses and casual garments. The main vest (see page 66) was made from double-knitted jersey and the sister vest (see page 74) from light cotton jersey.

Lace a delicate fabric stitched into beautiful shapes used for overlaying or decorating garments. Either hand made or machine sewn, lace is made from yarn or thread in either silk, gold or silver thread or cotton. **Best for:** dressy pieces and adding embelishments.

Lawn a sheer, lightweight cotton fabric that is slightly transparent. **Best for:** lightweight dresses, blouses, skirts and trousers; it would work well for the main blouse (see page 144), sister dress (see page 110), the sister trousers (see page 133) and the culottes (see page 142).

Leather technically not a fabric, leather is a natural material made from treated animal skin. **Best for:** coats, dresses, skirts and trousers; it would work well for the shift

dress (see page 100) and skirt (see page 80).

Linen made from the flax plant and twice as strong as cotton, linen gets softer with washing and tends to crease due to its low elasticity. **Best for:** summer garments and inexperienced sewers. The sister blouse (see page 157) would work well in linen, along with the sister trousers (see page 133).

Lycra® a synthetic fibre, Lycra® is the brand name for spandex. It's a strong, durable and elastic fabric added to many fabrics to give added stretch. **Best for:** skintight clothing such as leggings and leotards.

Lyocell a sustainable fabric constructed from wood pulp. It's a soft, lightweight, breathable and crease-resistant fabric that drapes beautifully. **Best for:** dresses and skirts; the sister shift dress (see page 110) and sister skirt (see page 92) would work well.

Moleskin a soft, hard-wearing, medium-weight fabric, moleskin is a good alternative to wool or linen and comes in a wide range of brilliant colours. **Best for:** winter trousers and jackets; it would work well on the wiggle skirt (see page 99) and the main trousers (see page 122).

Muslin a loosely woven, lightweight cotton fabric that drapes well and is ideal for dyeing. **Best for:** lightweight dresses, blouses, skirts and trousers; it would work well for the sister blouse (see page 157) and maxi skirt (see page 96).

Nylon made from a strong, stretchy fibre, nylon is one of the most useful and versatile synthetic fabrics. **Best for:** outdoor clothing, jackets and bags because it dries quickly.

Organza produced from highly twisted yarn, this has a crisp, sheer finish. It can be made from silk or synthetic fibres. **Best for:** more formal, dressy pieces including bridal wear.

Polyester made from synthetic fibre, polyester is a very durable, crease-resistant fabric. **Best for:** casualwear including dresses, blouses and skirts. Polyester poplin would work well for the main shift dress (see page 100), the sister blouse (see page 157) and the

sister trousers (see page 133). The main blouse (see page 144) is made from polyester crepe de chine.

Poplin a plain-dyed, woven cotton fabric that is strong and versatile. It comes in light and medium weights. **Best for:** skirts, dresses and blouses; it would work well for the sister shift dress (see page 110), sister skirt (see page 92) and the main and sister blouses (see pages 144 and 157).

Sateen woven in the same way as traditional satin, cotton sateen is a medium-weight fabric with a lustrous look. **Best for:** party pieces.

Satin woven to produce a soft, medium-weight fabric with considerable sheen. Satin is traditionally made from silk, but can be made from cotton and many other fibres. It drapes beautifully. **Best for:** elegant wedding wear and party dresses; it would work well for the sister dress (see page 110) the blouse with the pussy bow for 80s-inspired glamour (see page 164).

Tulle a delicate, net fabric made from nylon, polyester,

silk or cotton. **Best for:** completing a garment that requires a sheer lacy element.

Twill a heavyweight fabric made from cotton or linen with a weave that creates distinctive diagonal ribs. It is durable and crease- and water-resistant. **Best for:** winter garments; it would work well on the main trousers (see page 122) and main shift dress (see page 100).

Velvet an elegant, medium-weight fabric with a pile and a distinctive soft feel. It can be made from silk, cotton or synthetic fibres, and drapes beautifully. **Best for:** evening wear; it would work well on the main trousers (see page 122) or the shift dress for special occasions (see page 100).

Wool is a natural fibre, including alpaca, angora, cashmere, mohair and lambswool. It produces a soft, versatile fabric that is warm in winter and cool in summer. **Best for:** a wide range of clothing including coats, dresses, skirts and trousers. The sister trousers (see page 133) are made from a blend of wool and cashmere.

FINISH

In this chapter we'll be focusing on choices and techniques for garment construction and decorative touches. This includes choosing the most appropriate stitching for your garment and getting the best seam finishes, as well as looking at fastenings options and pocket styles.

Stitching

Stitching is the most important element in garment construction and it's essential that you choose the right stitch. Some stitching is meant to be visible while other types should be almost invisible. We have listed the best stitching options for each project and here we show you how to do them.

HAND STITCHING

Although many sewers now prefer to machine stitch, all garments can be hand sewn. Hand stitching can improve accuracy by giving you control of the fabric and can give a lovely professional finish. Invest in good-quality needles and thread, as these will make a big difference to your sewing experience.

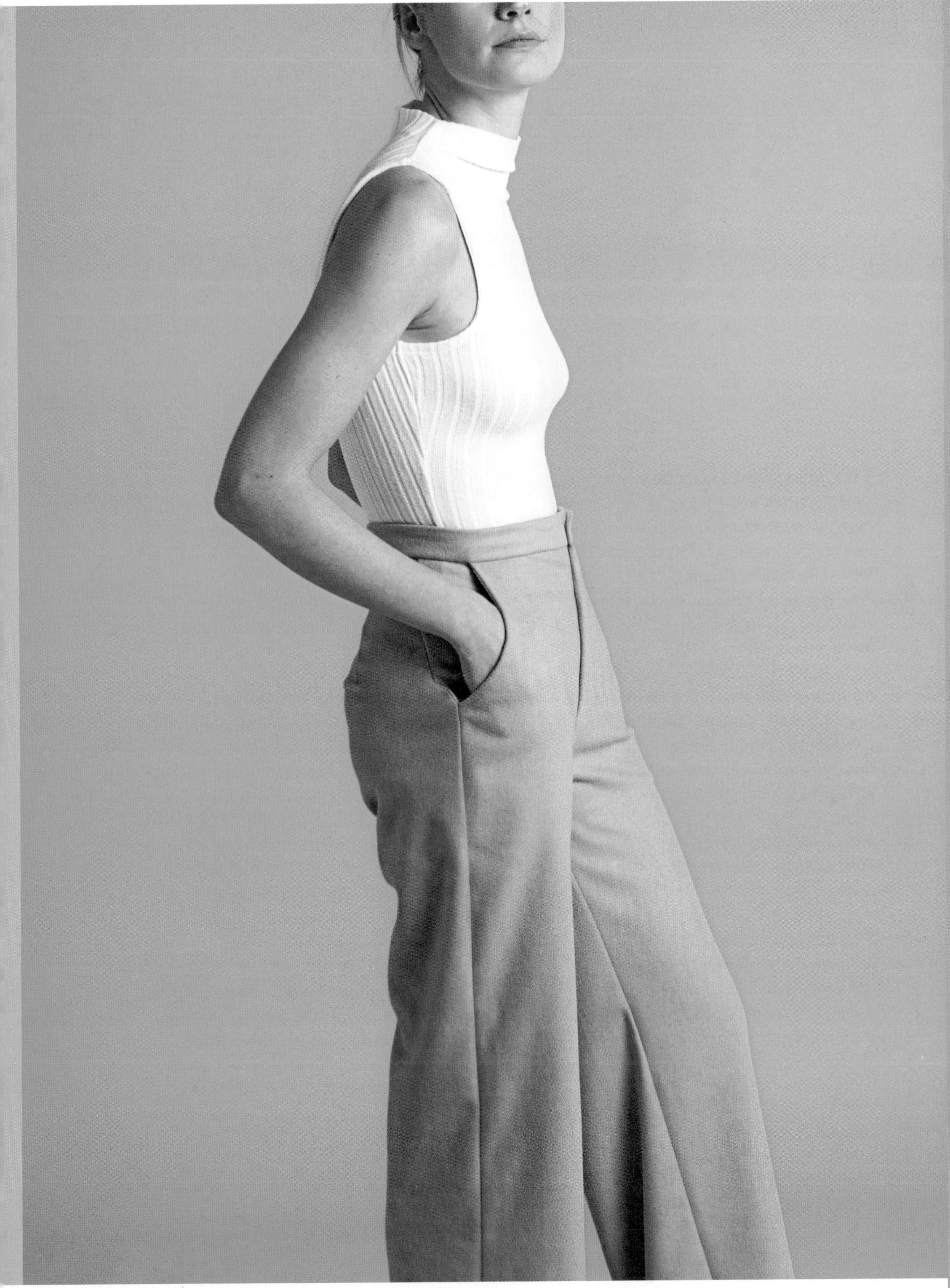

Five great hand stitches

Running stitch: *Small stitches of equal length.* Push the needle up through the fabric so the gaps are the same length as the stitches. Repeat. **Variation: Tacking (basting)**: *Work in the same way as for running stitch but make longer stitches, so they are easier to pull out when no longer needed.*

Back stitch: *This strong stitch can be used for sewing, mending seams and hemming.*
1 Working from left to right push the needle into the fabric to anchor the stitch with the knot on the wrong side of the fabric.

2 Then over 6mm to the right of the anchoring point and push the needle up, pulling the thread taut.

3 Now go back on yourself just under half way and push the needle into the fabric. Then over again 6mm to the right of the previous stitch and push the needle up, pulling the thread taut. Repeat. One side will have threads overlapping and the other side will be a line of small dashes.

Half slip stitch: *This invisible stitch is used for seams and hems.*
1 Working from right to left, bring the needle up from the wrong side through to the fold.

2 Take the needle through one or two threads of the bottom layer of fabric just above the fold and pull the thread through.

3 Push the needle back into the top layer through the fold, travel it about 1.25cm, then pull it back out through the fold. Repeat.

Slip stitch/ladder stitch: *This is used to sew two folds together – for instance on lining.*
1 Bring the needle and thread through the bottom fold, bring the needle out and pierce the top fold parallel to the underneath stitch.

2 Pass the thread through, then repeat with the bottom fold, etc – this will hide the thread. By sewing in parallel, you won't see the stitch at all. If you sew diagonally you'll see little stitches across the top layer of fabric.

Herringbone stitch: *Perfect for hand stitching hems as it's almost invisible from the right side.*
1 Finish off the raw edge, by either edge finishing the raw edge or tucking the raw edge under. Starting from the left, pull the needle up through the fold of the hem and anchor in place with a backstitch.

2 Make a long diagonal stitch to the right or

Running stitch

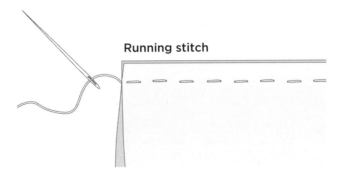

Slip stitch/ladder stitch

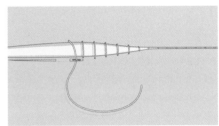

Back stitch

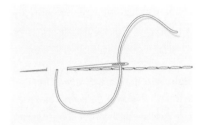

Herringbone stitch

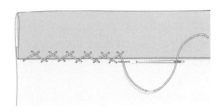

Half slip stitch

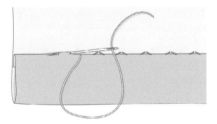

through the edge finished edge, catching one or two threads in the bottom layer of fabric from right to left.

3 Make another long diagonal stitch to the right, this time pushing the needle through just the top layer of hem from right to left. Repeat, making sure the stitches are even.

4 Make the final stitch into the hem and secure on the wrong side.

Three ways to thread a needle

The perfect length of thread is based on a 'tailor's measure', which usually avoids knotting and other problems. A tailor's measure is roughly an arm's length (about 80cm), so pull the thread from the spool so that your arm is stretched out to the side before snipping the thread.

Single thread: Thread a tailor's measure of thread through the eye of the needle. Knot the cut end if you wish. **Best for:** hemming, seams.

Single thread doubled over: Use a double tailor's measure. Thread the needle so the two threads are the same length and tie a knot in the cut end. **Best for:** sewing on buttons and fastenings.

Double thread: Use a double tailor's measure. Fold the thread in half, thread the eye of the needle with the looped end, then pull the loop through so it is longer than the cut end. **Best for** stitching that needs to be particularly durable, such as sewing on buttons, or hooks and eyes and other fastening. Also by bringing the first stitch through the loop, the stitch is anchored in place neatly and easily.

STRENGTHENING THREAD
To make your thread more robust and prevent knotting, run it through beeswax. Then rub the thread between finger and thumb or press it with a warm iron to seal the wax in.

Zigzag

MACHINE STITCHING

Your sewing machine will undoubtedly have a wide range of adjustable stitches. We have selected four stitches for this book.

Straight stitch: *A universal machine setting, straight stitch is used for seams and topstitching.* Set the stitch length to 2.3–2.6 (this can change depending on the fabric and amount of layers.

Tacking (basting) stitch: *These long stitches quickly and temporarily secure fabric in place.* Set to the longest length on your machine.

Zigzag stitch: *A zigzag finish can be used on almost any seam to enclose the raw edge. You can vary the stitch width and length to help maintain a smooth seam. Shorter stitches work best on lighter fabrics, longer ones for heavier fabrics. It's also a good stitch to use on stretch fabrics.* Place the middle of the foot over the raw edge of fabric, so that the stitch encases the edge. Alternatively, zigzag close to the edge, then trim away the excess.

Blind hem stitch: *If you have a blind stitch foot, this stitch will give an invisible finish to hems.*
1 To use the blind hem foot, you need to fold the fabric correctly. Fold the hem allowance once, wrong sides together, and press. With the fabric right side down and the garment to the left of the machine foot, fold the hem under, right sides together and leaving 6mm of the hem allowance visible.

Blind hem stitch

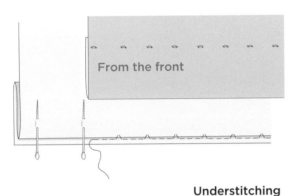

From the front

Overlocker

Understitching

**Blind hem
machine symbol**

2 Slide the hem under the blind hem foot with the folded edge butting up to the metal guide. Set the machine to blind hem stitch. Sew the hem; the stitch will catch the folded edge every couple of stitches. Once finished, unfold the hem and press.

Using an overlocker

An overlocker is a specialised type of sewing machine that stitches, cuts and finishes raw edges. It uses three, four or five threads to create a looped effect that encases the raw edge and prevents fraying. It's a fast finishing technique and brilliant for sewing stretch fabrics.
Overlock along the raw edge, aligning the cut edge with your overlock blade.

Stitches for different purposes

Staystitching: *This stitch prevents stretching on areas that are cut on the bias.*
Sew a straight, single line of stitches, on the machine or by hand, on a single layer of fabric,

approximately 5mm from the edge. Eventually, the staystitching may be trimmed away with the seam allowance.

Topstitching: *Visible on the right side of the garment, this type of stitching is used for functional and decorative purposes.*
On the right side, sew stitches close together by hand or, on the machine, use a slightly longer stitch length to sew a single, straight line of stitches. Use the edge of the fabric as a guide or, for more decorative topstitching, follow your own markings.

Understitching: *This type of stitching can be seen on the inside of a garment and is used to prevent a lining or facing coming up over the top of the seamline.*
Using backstitch by hand or a normal-length straight stitch on the machine, sew the facing or lining to the seam allowance underneath, close to the seam edge.

Seams

In dressmaking there are several ways to sew two pieces of fabric together to create strong and beautiful seams. Think about where your seams sit and if they are going to be seen as part of the aesthetic of the garment. A seam allowance is essential for strong seams as sewing directly to the edge of cut fabric will weaken the seam and cause fraying. Once a seam is finished careful pressing allows the seam to be shaped and controlled and the thread to fully merge with the fabric.

Straight stitched seam

This seam is the most commonly used.
It is sewn with a straight stitch 1.5cm from the fabric edge, right sides together. Choose the stitch length according to the thickness of the fabric.

French seam

A French seam completely encases the raw edges, giving a lovely couture finish. For this reason, use French seams on garments where the seams will be visible.

1 With the fabric pieces wrong sides together and the edges lined up, stitch 5mm from the edge.

2 Trim the seam allowances to about 3mm. Press both seam allowances to one side.

3 Fold right sides together and stitch the seam again with a 1cm seam allowance, encasing the raw edges. Press the seam allowance to one side.

Flat fell seam

All the edges on this seam are encased on the right side and sewn flat. It's durable, sturdy and looks very neat. It's commonly used for jeans.

1 With wrong sides together, sew the seam, using a 1.5cm seam allowance. Press both seam allowances to one side.

2 Trim the bottom seam allowance to half the width and fold under the raw edge of the top seam allowance so that it meets the stitching line and press.

French seam

Flat fell seam

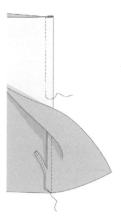
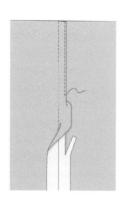

Edge finishes

A seam isn't complete until you apply an edge finish. Finishing a seam keeps it secure and prevents the fabric fraying. Well-finished seams make the inside of your garments as neat and polished as the outside, improving the quality and longevity.

Pinked edging

This technique works best on fabrics that don't fray easily. Pinking shears have sawtooth blades, which cut a zigzag edge on the fabric, helping to prevent fraying.

Trim the raw edges with pinking shears after sewing each seam.

Zigzag stitching

A stitched zigzag finish can be used on almost any seam to enclose the raw edges and prevent fraying.

1 Select zigzag stitch and stitch width and length to suit the weight of the fabric. Smaller stitches work best for lighter fabrics and longer stitches for heavier fabrics. It's a good idea to test the stitch on a scrap of the same fabric to check it stays as a smooth seam and doesn't create extra bulk.

2 Place the raw edge of the fabric under the foot either so that the stitch will encase the edge or so that the stitch is close to the edge and the excess can be trimmed away. You can either zigzag each seam allowance separately or join the two allowances for each together. It's better to do it separately for bulkier fabrics.

Turn under

This neat tailored finish works well on light- to medium-weight fabrics.

Turn under 3mm along the raw edge of the seam allowance, or 6mm if the fabric frays easily. Press. Straight stitch along the folded edge.

TOP TIP FOR TURNING EDGES UNDER

When working with fine fabrics or curved edges, sew a line of stitches along the foldline to help turn the edge under.

- - - - - - - - - - - - - -

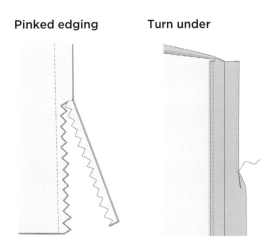

Pinked edging   **Turn under**

Bias binding

Bias binding is cut from fabric on the diagonal. This gives it stretch, so it lies flat when applied to garment edges. It provides a functional finish, binding raw edges, or can be purely decorative, for example, accentuating a hemline with a contrasting colour or fabric. A wide range of bias binding widths and colours is available to buy, or you could make your own.

1 Line up the right side of the fabric raw edge with the right side of the bias binding. Pin.

2 Stitch along the fold on the binding, removing the pins as you go.

3 Fold the binding over the raw edge of fabric to the wrong side of the fabric.

4 Pin the remaining fold of the binding to the fabric. Topstitch or hand stitch along the folded edge to secure the binding. Press. Alternatively press the bias binding in half and fold it over the raw edge. Sew everything in place near the fold of the bias binding for a quick tidy finished edge.

Overlocking a seam

An overlocking machine cuts the fabric and stitches 3, 4 or 5 threads around the edge creating a looped effect that prevents fraying. It's a fast finishing technique. Overlock along the raw edge of the hem, aligning the cut edge with your overlock blade.

Bias binding

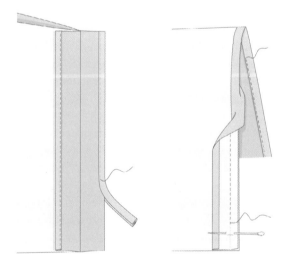

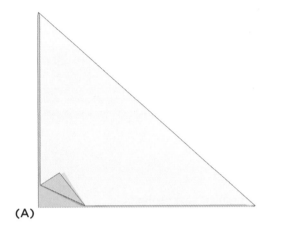

(A)

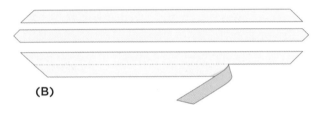

(B)

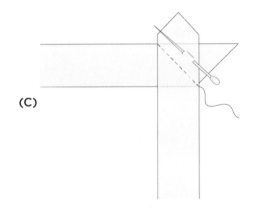

(C)

TOP TIP FOR BIAS BINDING
Consider the sequence in which you join
shorter and longer lengths together. You
might be able to plan ahead so that the
joins can be positioned on the garment
where they are least noticeable and
create least bulk.

MAKE YOUR OWN BIAS BINDING

This method turns a large square of fabric into
bias binding with very little waste.

1 Decide on the width of the binding you want
and how much you need for your project, for
example for 1cm wide binding. Multiply this by
four; in our example, this would be 4cm.

2 Fold a square piece of fabric diagonally and
press the fold lightly. Open out the square. **(A)**

3 Using a ruler, measure and pencil mark a
line, 4cm from and parallel to the pressed line.
Continue to measure 4cm widths across the rest
of the fabric square.

4 Following the pencil lines, cut the fabric into
4cm strips **(B)**. Straighten the ends of the strips.

5 Pin two strips, at right angles, right sides
together. Sew diagonally across the overlapped
square shape. **(C)**

6 Trim the seam allowance and press open.
Repeat, to add as many strips together as
you need.

7 Fold the bias strip in half lengthways, wrong
sides together, and press lightly. Open out and
fold each raw edge to the centre fold and press
firmly.

8 Alternatively, use a bias tape maker to fold the
binding. Push the fabric strip through the bias
tape maker wrong side up, if necessary easing
the end of the fabric into the opening with a
seam ripper. Pull the strip through to give a
single fold bias binding.

Hems

After all the measuring, cutting and sewing, the final big decision is your choice of hem. There are no set rules when it comes to hemming and the best place to start is to take inspiration from your favourite garments in your wardrobe.

HEM WIDTHS

NARROW HEMS (3MM/6MM)

work well with lighter, mid-weight fabrics and floaty patterns as it allows the fabric to move more effortlessly.

MID-WIDTH HEMS (1.25CM)

add structure to blouses and dresses.

WIDE HEMS (2.5CM)

enhances the hang in medium weight fabrics and gives a solid finish to more relaxed trousers, skirts and dresses.

THICK HEMS (3CM/5CM)

Added to the bottom of tailored dresses and skirts, these allow the garment to drape properly.

Double hem

Double folded hems work brilliantly with light to medium-weight woven fabrics.

1 Press the raw edge under by 6mm, then make a second fold in line with the raw edge if wanting a narrow hem, or your own desired distance if wanting a wider hem.

2 Machine or hand stitch the hem in place.

Single hem

Single fold hems work best for thick woven fabrics as a double hem may be too bulky.

1 Finish the raw edge first. Then fold the edge over and press.

2 Machine or hand stitch the hem in place.

Single hem

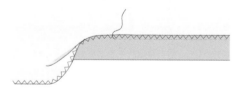

Double hem

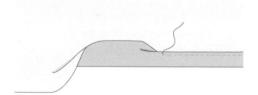

Rolled hem

A rolled hem is very narrow and creates a beautiful finish. They work best on lightweight and delicate woven fabrics and also on any circular hem. Rolling a hem takes a little practice and patience, by hand or on the machine, but persevere and you'll love the results.

Machine-rolled hem

You'll need a rolled hem presser foot, which has a curled part that rolls the fabric over as you stitch. Rolled hems can make the fabric kink and curl, especially on a circular piece of fabric, so pressing is essential.

1 With the wrong side up, finger press the raw edge over. Turn another fold and pin to keep the first few centimetres of rolled edge in place.

2 Fit the rolled hem presser foot on the machine and set to straight stitch.

3 Position the fabric under the foot, aligning the edge of the hem with the guide on the foot.

4 Sew a couple of stitches to secure the thread.

5 Raise the foot with the needle down in the fabric. Tuck the folded hem into the curl of the foot.

6 Lower the foot and begin sewing. Lift the edge of the fabric slightly so it glides over the curl as you stitch, rolling the fabric and creating a neat hem.

Alternatively, if you haven't got a rolled hem foot, simply fold the fabric over into a single mini hem, press and stitch in place. Press the mini fold

Machine-rolled hem

Hand rolled hem

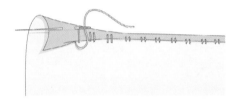

again over your stitch line. You'll see your initial stitch line on the wrong side. Sew over this stitch line and press. You'll only see one line of stitching on the right side of the fabric.

Hand-stitched rolled hem

This neat rolled hem, with minimal visible stitching, is created using a stitch similar to a half slipstitch.

1 Working on the wrong side, secure a length of matching thread. Then take the needle to the right side about 3mm from the raw edge.

2 Roll the raw edge towards the wrong side, using the needle tip to keep the raw edge under, so that your first stitch now sits at the top of the fold.

3 Make a tiny stitch catching one or two threads of the main garment fabric, close to the first stitch in the hem. Pull the thread through.

Fastenings

Fastenings can be both functional and decorative. They make it possible to get in and out of a garment, while retaining the desired fitting, and can also enhance and embellish. The fastenings need to work in harmony with the garment design and often hidden fastenings are the best option. However, an exposed zipper can add an edgy touch to a dress and patterned buttons can make a simple blouse zing.

ZIPPERS

Mastering zips is an essential skill as a poorly inserted zip will scream homemade. There are four main choices: invisible, concealed, exposed and fly, and the key to successsful insertion is all about preparation to ensure the zipper is centred correctly.

Inserting an invisible zipper

You'll need a length of 'invisible' zipper and an invisible zipper foot to produce a professional invisible zipper fastening. You also need to insert the zipper before sewing the rest of the seam.

1 Open the invisible zipper and place it right side down on the right side of the fabric, aligning the teeth with the seamline. The edge of the tape should be parallel with the raw edge of the fabric but keeping a few millimetres of the fabric visible so it doesn't sneak under the zipper. Pin the first side of the zipper in place. **(A)**

2 Put the zipper under the invisible zipper foot with the zipper teeth in the channel on the foot. Pushing the teeth to the side, sew along the zipper as close to the teeth as you can. The teeth will coil back. **(B)**

3 Position the other side of the zipper on the second piece of fabric in a similar way, right sides together. Pin the zipper in place, then practise zipping it up to make sure it is positioned correctly and looks good from the right side. Unzipper and sew the zipper in place as before.

4 Close the zipper. Working on the wrong side of the fabric, pin the seam allowances together underneath the zipper. Pin the rest of the seam.

5 Using a regular zipper foot, start stitching the seam with the side of the foot slightly above the end of the zipper. Continue to about 5cm past the end of the zipper. Sew as close to the stitch line as you can so there are no puckers around the bottom of the zipper. **(C & D)**

6 Change the foot to your regular presser foot and continue to sew the rest of the seam.

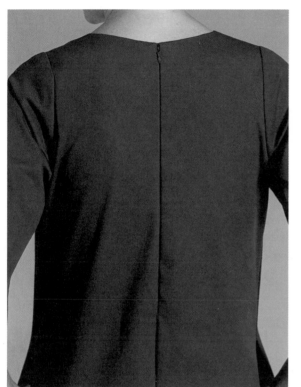

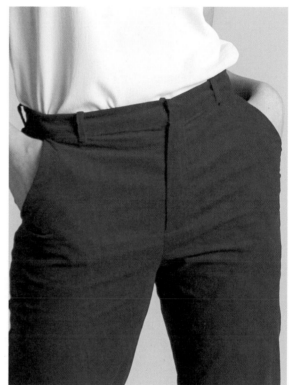

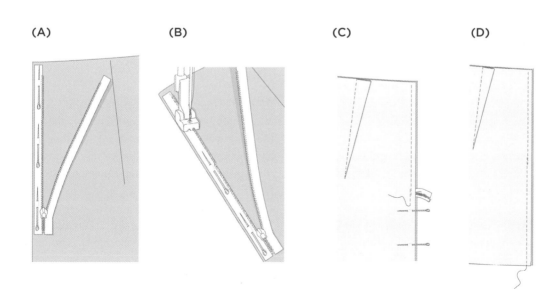

(A)   (B)   (C)   (D)

Inserting a concealed zipper

In this method, you'll insert the zipper from the right side, so you can keep the stitches nice and even. You'll need a regular zipper foot.

1 On the fabric, mark where you want the bottom end of the zipper to sit.

2 Select a long straight tacking (basting) stitch on your machine and start to sew the seam, right sides together, from the top of the garment to the notch. The long stitch will be easier to unpick when you need to do so later.

3 At the notch, select a regular length stitch, back stitch a little to secure and sew the rest of the seam.

4 Press the seam allowances open and finish the raw edges individually.

5 With the fabric pieces face down, place the zipper onto the seam allowance with the zipper teeth face down along the seam. Pin, then tack (baste) the zipper in place. **(A)**

6 Using the zipper foot and keeping the zipper closed, place the zipper under the foot, slightly past the zipper head. The zipper foot will happily hug the teeth of the zipper but you can't sew around the head as it protrudes too much.

7 Sew down the length of the zipper. When you get near the end, stop with the needle down, lift the foot and sew across the zipper teeth. Your machine should happily sew over plastic teeth; if using a metal zipper, be sure to sew over the tape and not the teeth.

8 Sew up the other side of the zipper. When you reach the point that corresponds to the start on the other side, leave the needle down and push the zipper head down past the zipper foot. Continue sewing to the end. **(B)**

9 With the zipper head still pushed down, return back to the first side and sew from the top down to the original start point. You should have smooth parallel stitch lines. Pull the loose threads through to the wrong side and tie in a knot to secure. **(C)**

10 On the right side, remove the tacking stitches to open the seam and reveal the zipper. **(D)**

**TOP TIP FOR INSERTING
AN INVISIBLE ZIPPER**
All the stitching is done on the
wrong side, hidden within the
seam allowance, which makes an
invisible zipper one of the easiest
to insert.

(A)

(B)

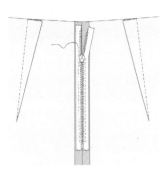

(C)

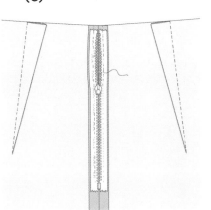

(D)

Inserting a fly zipper
As well as a regular zipper foot, you'll need some iron-on interfacing to create a fly zipper.

1 Cut out your garment, including the notches, snips and tailor tacks. On both the left and the right leg, draw a chalk line from the snip to the tail tack, right side up. On the right leg piece, draw another line parallel to this, 2.5cm long (towards the edge of the fly) and chalk this in. **(A)** Be aware of which is the left and and which the right leg piece – it is how you wear them rather than how they are laid out in front of you.

2 Place the zipper right side down so the raw edge meets the dashed line.

3 Pin and sew the zipper to the fly, close to the line. Sew a parallel line closer to the zipper teeth moving the zipper up and down to get a smooth line of stitching. **(B)**

4 Place the left trouser leg piece underneath the right leg piece, rights sides together. Fold back the right side fly extension with the zipper on it so that the zipper lies flat on the

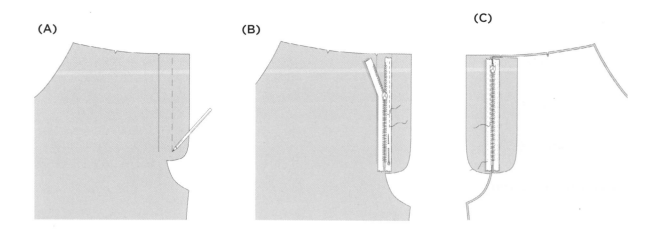

(A)   (B)   (C)

left fly. Match up the notches, snips, etc. Pin and sew in place with two parallel lines as before. **(C)**

5 With your zipper in place, sew the trousers together from the tailor tacks to the inside leg seam around the curve. It helps having the zipper unzipped here.

6 Clip to the tailor tack on the left leg only. **(D)**

7 Right side up, place the left centre fold over the zipper (the fold should match up with the original chalk line). Finger press flat, than pin in place. **(E)**

8 Measure 3.5cm from centre fold and chalk in a line finishing off with a nice curve to meet the bottom of the fly opening. Topstitch in place.

9 Fold the fly guard right side together. Pin and sew along the bottom edge. Trim away any excess. Pull through to the right side and press.

10 Place the fly guard over the zipper on the wrong side of the trousers, matching up the folded edge against the left leg fly. Pin the raw edges to the right fly (the right fly will be slightly wider). Pin and stitch the fly guard to the right fly only, trim away excess and finish edge. **(F)**

11 On the right side with the fly guard flat underneath the zipper, secure all the layers in place with a topstitch, sewing as close as you can to the zipper. Sew with the zipper down. **(G)**

(D) **(E)**

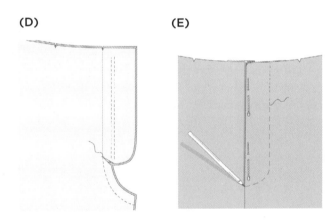

(F) **(G)**

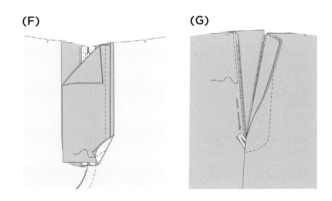

Inserting an exposed zipper

Exposed zippers come in different lengths and colours, so you can match or complement your garment. The zipper teeth are made of metal or chunky plastic. You'll also need light- or medium-weight interfacing to stabilise your fabric. Roughly twice the width of the zipper and 2.5cm longer than the zipper tape will be sufficient. Exposed zippers can be inserted with or without a seam.

1 Fuse the interfacing on the wrong side of fabric, so the long edges are equal distances from where the zipper line will be.

2 On the interfacing, draw a straight line down the zipper line to where the bottom end of the zipper teeth will sit.

3 Draw a horizontal line across the zipper line just beyond where the zipper stopper will be. **(A)**

4 Metal zipper teeth usually measure 1cm across and the opening in the fabric needs to match this measurement so that the teeth are exposed. You could adapt this if you also want to see some of the tape. For a 1cm opening, sew a line of stitches 5mm away from and all the way round the marked zipper line. **(B)**

5 Cut down the zipper line to the horizontal mark. Then cut diagonally into the corners of the stitch line, taking care not to snip through the stitches. **(C)**

6 Fold the fabric to the wrong side along the stitch line and press. **(D)**

7 Working from the right side, place the zipper in the opening, lining everything up. Pin, then tack (baste) the zipper in place, making sure you secure the tape to the seam allowance. **(E)**

8 Using a zipper foot and moving the zipper head as necessary, sew the zipper in place close to the folded edges **(F)**. Remove the basting (tacking) stitches. **(G)**

**TOP TIP FOR
AN EXPOSED ZIP**
Cleverly placing an exposed zip along the side seam of a fitted shift dress can help to mininise the waistline

- - - - - - - - - - - - -

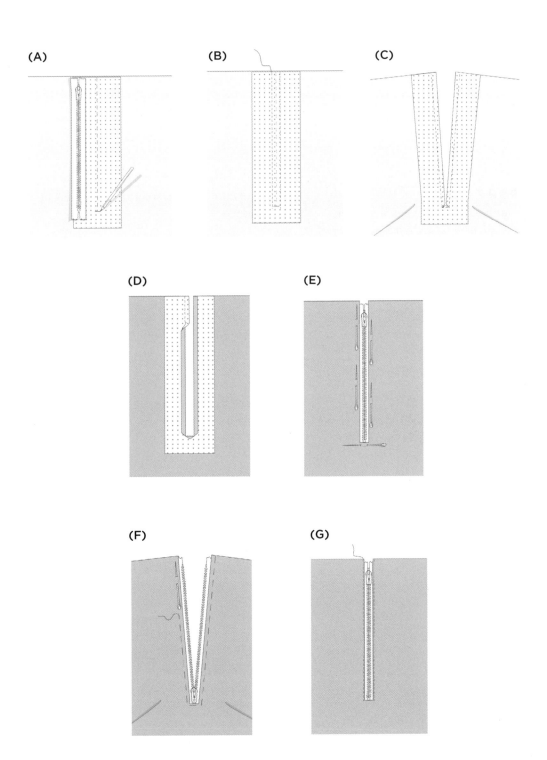

(A)

(B)

(C)

(D)

(E)

(F)

(G)

POPPERS

Poppers are usually round or square in shape, made of plastic or metal and come in an array of sizes. They work in pairs, known as the male and female components. One part snaps into place inside the other to make a secure fastening.

1 Place the two relevant parts of the garment together. Mark where you want the popper to go, then pierce through the layers with a pin. Mark the position for the popper on all the layers. **(A)**

2 The male component should go on the wrong side of the part of the garment that will sit on top of the other part. Secure a length of double thread.

3 Holding the popper in place, bring the needle up through one of the holes in the popper and anchor it in place by taking the needle back through the fabric. **(B)**

4 Secure the popper with three or four stitches through each holes. Fasten off.

5 Repeat with the female component, positioning that on the right side of the other part of the garment.

(A)

(B)

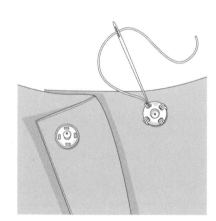

(A)

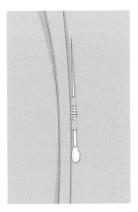

(B)

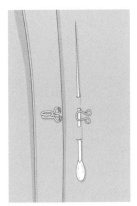

HOOKS AND EYES

These little metal gizmos also work in pairs. There's a hook and a bar called an eye. The hook fits into the eye to secure the closure.

1 The hook should go on the wrong side of the part of the garment that will sit on top of the other part. Mark where it will go so the top of the hook will be close to the edge of the fabric.

2 Secure a length of double thread where it cannot be seen and bring the thread up close to the mark.

3 Holding the hook in place, take the needle through one of the loops, then anchor it in place by taking the needle back through the fabric. Repeat three more times.

4 Tunnel your needle between the layers of fabric to the base of the hook, secure the hook in place with a couple of stitches then tunnel the needle back to the other metal loop and repeat step 3.

5 Fasten off with a few tiny stitches. Run the thread between the layers of fabric and snip the end where it won't be seen.

6 With the relevant garment pieces together, fold the fabric to expose the hook. Place a pin underneath the hook and through the fabric layers to mark the placement for the eye. **(A & B)**

7 Secure the thread and then the eye in the same way as for the hook, making sure the eye is really secure and won't wiggle around. Fasten off in the same way.

BUTTONS

Buttons come in many different sizes and styles and as well as being used to join fabrics together, they work well as ornamental features.

Making a buttonhole

Following your sewing machine's buttonholes instructions, mark up on your garment where you want your buttons to go and sew as directed.

Sewing on a button

1 Thread your needle to match your button, using double thread or single thread doubled over (see page 38).

2 Mark on the position for the button, using the buttonhole as a guide. Secure the thread on the inside of the garment, close to the button position.

3 Thread the button onto the needle and stitch it in place, neatly up and down through the holes. Tilt the button slightly so that there is a little bit of space between the fabric and the button. Stitch five to eight times, depending on how robust the garment needs to be.

4 After the final stitch, come up underneath the button and wrap the thread round the slightly looser stitches underneath the button to create a shank, which will enable the button to move. If you are working with heavier fabric, you need to ensure that this doesn't pull and pucker the fabric. Using the same method, incorporate a matchstick or hairgrip on top of the button and sew over, this leaves a bit more extra space between the fabric and the button, making it more moveable **(A)**. Before winding the thread around the stitches, remove the matchstick or hairgrip and lift the button up to give more space for wrapping. **(B)**

(A)

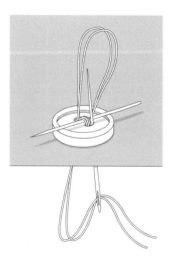

(B)

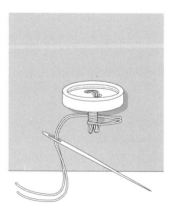

Making button loops

Also known as crochet loops, this type of button fastening is a really handy alternative to a buttonhole. You can also adapt it to make a smaller version that will work as an eye.

1 Begin by sewing your button in place, as this will indicate how long the loop needs to be.

2 Double thread a needle in a colour to match the fabric. Secure the thread on the wrong side of the part of the garment that needs to fasten to the button.

3 Bring the thread to the position for the button loop. Make a stitch to create a loop of thread. **(A)**

4 Hold the loop open with your thumb and forefinger so there are two threads on each side and grab the thread from the needle with your thumb and forefinger from your other hand. Pull the thread through the loop to create a knot at the base. **(B)**

5 Repeat to make a chain of the desired length. Then push the needle through the thread loop to secure the end.

6 Catch the fabric with the needle where you want to position the end of the loop. Bring the needle through until the end of the new loop meets the fabric. Secure with a few stitches and hide the thread within the layers of fabric before snipping the ends.

7 Secure the thread on the wrong side of the garment.

(A)

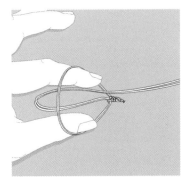

(B)

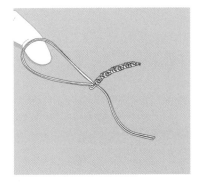

Pockets

Whether it's hidden away in the side seam or added to a garment as a visible statement, a pocket is a lovely addition to any item of clothing. It's also very practical! There are lots of variations and we've chosen four of our favourites.

Patch pockets

A patch pocket is a separate piece of fabric sewn onto the outside of a garment.

1 Cut the pocket piece from the fabric.

2 Fold the fabric over 2.5cm, right sides together. Then fold up the raw edge by 6mm. This is the top of the pocket. Press.

3 Sew down both top edges of the pocket, along each seamline, securing both folds at each end. **(A)**

4 Trim excess fabric from both top corners.

5 Turn the pocket top right sides out and poke each corner out to a nice sharp point. Press. Pin, then topstitch the turned hem in place close to the folded edge. Press. **(B)**

6 Fold under the rest of the raw edges, by 6mm down the sides and by 1cm across the bottom of the pocket. To get a crisp, professional finish, mitre the bottom turning at each corner by folding the fabric at a right angle. Press, pin, then baste (tack) in place. **(C)**

7 Pin the pocket in place on the main fabric piece. **(D)**

8 Sew on the pocket, close to the edges. Start by sewing a long triangle at the top of the pocket. Continue sewing down the side, across the bottom and up the other side, finishing with a similar triangle.

9 Remove basting (tacking) stitches and press.

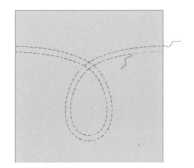

TOP TIP
DESIGNING
PATCH POCKETS

You can make patch pockets in a wide range of shapes – a diamond shape or a scalloped or curved edge work swell. You can use the same principles to make any of these.

- - - - - - - - - - - - -

DECORATING PATCH POCKETS

A decorated back pocket can have a huge impact and is easy to do before applying the pocket to the garment. Use any design, from simple lines to an embroidered motif. Look online or in shops for inspiration.

1 Transfer your design onto the pocket fabric, using an air-erasable pen, chalk or transfer paper. Make sure the design doesn't overlap into the seam allowances.

2 Fuse interfacing to the wrong side of the fabric to add strength.

3 Thread your sewing machine with your chosen colour and get stitching.

4 Press the pocket, then apply it to the garment in the usual way.

(A) **(B)**

(C) **(D)**

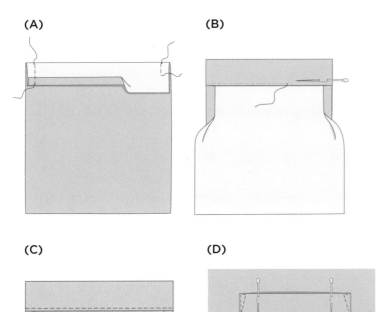

TOP TIP
FOR A CHUNKY LOOK

Thread your single needle with two threads for a chunkier look and even more impact. Great for jean hems too!

- - - - - - - - - - - - -

LAYERING SEAM ALLOWANCES

When working with multiple layers of fabric, it's important to layer the seam allowances, removing some of the excess fabric to reduce bulk and allow the garment to lay flat.

Grading the seam allowance
1 Sew the seam and press.

2 Beginning with the seam allowance furthest from the garment fabric, trim to 3mm–1cm from the stitching.

3 Trim the next layer of seam allowance a little wider.

4 Repeat this process on the other layers of seam allowance until the one nearest the garment fabric is trimmed to 6mm–1.5cm from the stitching.

Trim corners
For extra sharp corners on seams that meet at right angles or collars and waistbands, clip the corners to remove additional bulk.

Clip inner curves
For smooth necklines and curved seams, snip small triangles across the seam allowance to reduce the bulk of fabric.

Notch outer curves
For Peter Pan collars and outside curves, release the seam allowance by notching the outer curve to allow the fabric to have a smooth, even finish.

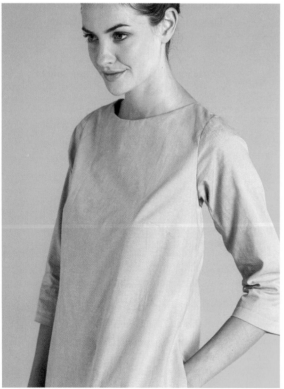

In-seam pockets

An in-seam pocket sits almost invisibly within the side seam of a garment. You can use the pattern piece from the shift dress, adapting the depth to suit your hand size if you wish.

1 Cut two pieces of fabric for each pocket and mark any notches.

2 Place one pocket piece on the main garment piece, right sides together and matching the notches. Pin. Make sure the curved end of the pocket piece points towards the hem of the garment. **(A)**

3 Repeat to attach the second pocket piece to the other main garment piece.

4 Sew the pocket pieces to the main garment pieces between the notches using 1cm seam allowance. Press.

5 Open out the pockets and press each seam. Understitch the seam allowances in place. **(B)**

6 Join the two main garment pieces, right sides together, using a 1.5cm seam allowance. Start by sewing the main garment seam from the top edge to the top pocket notch. Then sew around the raw edges of the pocket to the bottom pocket notch. Pivot, and continue sewing the main garment seam to the hem.

7 Snip carefully into the top and bottom pocket notches, without cutting the stitches. Press and finish the seam allowances. **(C)**

8 Turn the main garment right sides out, leaving the pocket inside. Press, before continuing the construct the rest of the garment.

(A)   **(B)**   **(C)**

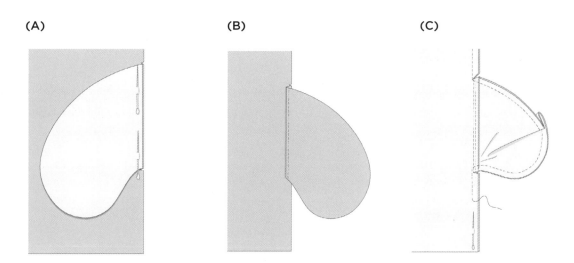

Diagonal pockets

With a visible diagonal opening, this type of pocket works well on trousers and skirts. You might want to use lightweight fusible interfacing to add body to the pocket opening. We used these pockets on our main trousers (page 122) and sister skirt (page 92).

1 Cut the pieces out of fabric. You should have your main garment piece, a pocket lining and a pocket piece.

2 Staystitch or use lightweight fusible interfacing on the opening edge of the pocket lining and edge of the pocket opening on the garment to prevent it stretching.

3 Place the pocket lining on top of the garment front, right sides together. Pin and sew in place, using a 1.5cm seam allowance. Clip the seam allowance to reduce bulk. **(A)**

4 Flip the pocket lining to the inside of the garment front and press the curved edge.

5 Understitch the pocket lining to the seam allowance to keep it in place. Press. **(B)**

6 With the garment wrong side up, place the pocket piece on top of the pocket lining, right sides together and matching the notches. Pin and sew around the curve of the pocket then edge finish the raw edge.

7 Flip the pocket underneath the garment and press the whole pocket flat. Topstitching along the pocket opening helps keep the pocket flat and adds a decorative edge. It depends on what

(A)

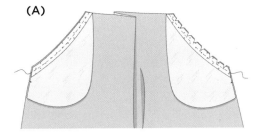

(B)

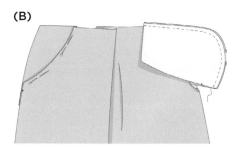

(C)

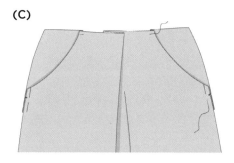

fabric you use for your garment. We didn't add this top-stitching to our yellow mini skirt due to the heavier weight fabric we used.

8 Making sure the pocket is laying flat, tack (baste) all three layers together in place along the waistline and down the side seam. It will be secured when you sew up the rest of the garment. **(C)**

Single welt pockets

This type of pocket sits horizontally on smart or formal garments and requires more precision to get a professional finish. There are two kinds, a single and a double welt pocket, as the names suggest, with one or two fabric strips sitting flush against the pocket opening. We have gone for a single welt pocket here, and adapted the tailoring to make them easier to sew while still giving great results.

For this type of pocket, you'll need some lightweight fusible interfacing, as well as some of your main fabric for the inside of the pocket and some lining.

We used single welt pockets on our trousers (page 128). We also used one extended pattern piece that will become the welt and the lining. If you want to use a lighter fabric for the pocket lining, make the welt out of your top fabric and the lining

out of something else. You will need to attach your lining to your welt.

1 Transfer the markings for the welt pocket opening to the wrong side of the main garment piece. If your garment has darts in the back, sew them in place first. Our trouser pattern has back darts.

2 Cut a piece of fabric for the welt. It needs to be 5cm wider than the pocket opening and your chosen depth of pocket, or use the trouser single welt pattern piece.

3 Cut a piece of fusible interfacing. It needs to be the same width as the welt fabric piece and approximately 6cm deep. Fuse it to the wrong side of your garment over the pocket markings. Transfer the marks and join the four corners together. You should have a rectangular box.

4 Place the welt piece underneath the garment, right sides together. The welt should be even on either side of the pocket markings and approximately 2.5cm above the top of the pocket marking. The bulk of the welt will be towards the hem. Pin. **(A, overleaf)**

5 Set your machine to a smaller stitch length of about 1.5 and carefully sew all the pieces together along the rectangular marked lines (this is the pocket opening). Don't reverse stitch to begin or end. Hand sew the loose end through to the wrong side and tie the loose ends in a knot. Snip off the excess.

6 Draw a horizontal line on the interfacing across the middle of the sewn box, stopping 1cm from the stitching at each end. Draw diagonal lines from each end into the corners.

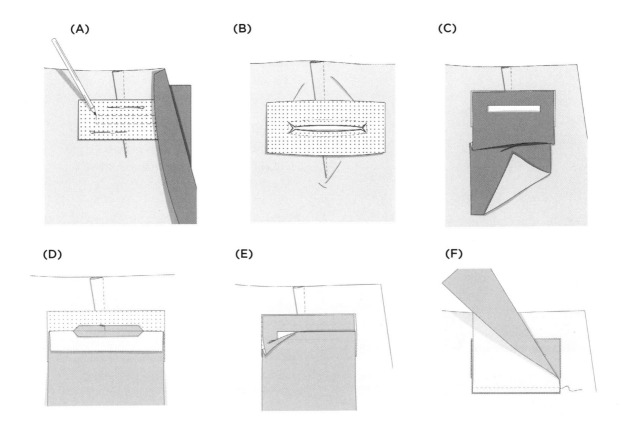

(A)

(B)

(C)

(D)

(E)

(F)

7 Cut along these lines and into the corners, as close to the stitching at the corners as possible without snipping through it. **(B)**

8 Turn the welt through the cut opening to the wrong side. Press. **(C)**

9 Along the top of the pocket opening, open out the seam allowance and press. Fold the welt piece along the seamline again and press. It should look nice and sharp. **(D)**

10 Repeat with the seam allowance along the bottom welt.

11 Working on the wrong side of the garment, pleat the welt pocket piece up to meet the top of the pocket opening. Press. **(E)**

If using an alternative pocket lining, cut a pocket lining the same width as the welt piece and about 25cm long. Pin, then sew the bottom edge of the welt to the short end of the pocket lining, right sides together and with a 1cm seam allowance. Press the seam allowance towards the welt. Pleat the welt as per step 11. **(F)**

12 Turning the garment over to the right side, pull back the garment revealing the pleat and the little triangle. Make sure the little triangle

(G)　　　　　　　　(H)　　　　　　　　(I)

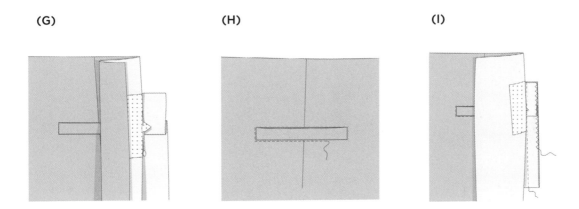

piece is pulled taught so the edge on the right side is sharp with no naughty bits poking out! Sew down the side of the pocket, over the pleat and triangle being careful not to sew on the main garment piece. Repeat on other side. **(G)**

13 On the right side of the garment, sew around the pocket opening either close to the edge or stitching in the ditch. Start at a corner and don't reverse stitch. Leave the threads long and loose. Take them through to the wrong side of the garment and tie securely. **(H)**

14 Fold the bottom edge of the pocket up to meet the top edge of the pocket piece, right

sides together. Pin together. Sew. Edge finish and press. **(I)**

15 Sew the top of the pocket lining close to the seam allowance underneath. Press.

THE VEST TOP

IN THIS CHAPTER YOU CAN MAKE:
The vest top (**page 72**)
Sister style: The lounge vest
(**page 74**)
A jersey dress (**page 78**)

Wonderfully versatile and ideal for everyday wear, this vest top is the perfect signature piece in the capsule collection. It's easy to make using a subtle stretch jersey fabric and the racer back detail adds a flattering shape across the shoulders. With no tricky fastenings, this vest top skims over curves for a beautifully close fit. If you prefer a looser fit, the lounge vest variation has greater ease for a more relaxed look and features a skinnier back detail.

Features of the vest top

MAIN STYLE

The vest is fitted, sleeveless and finishes just above the lower hip. It features:

- a scoop neck
- a racer back.

SISTER STYLE

The lounge vest has a relaxed fit, is sleeveless and finishes on the upper hip. It features:

- wider armholes
- a skinny back.

SUGGESTED FABRICS

This vest top works well in light- and medium-weight jersey. Avoid fabric that is very fine or has lots of stretch as it can be difficult to work with. We used double knit jersey in grey for the main vest and lightweight cotton jersey for the sister vest.

The vest top

Sister style: The lounge vest

Stone grey

Teal

Cotton jersey

Slate grey

Your pattern

The Vest Top has two pattern pieces.

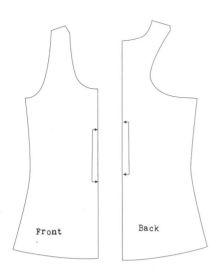

Front   Back

YOU WILL NEED TO CUT:

1 VEST FRONT ON THE FOLD
1 VEST BACK ON THE FOLD

Before you start

Take your measurements (see page 12) and then, if necessary, grade the pattern if you are between sizes (see page 16). We recommend making a toile before making the final garment (see page 18).

Your fabric layout

How the pattern pieces can be laid out on the jersey.

Back   Front

FABRIC QUANTITIES

Jersey usually only comes in the 140cm fabric width

SIZE	1–6
140cm	68cm/27"

THE VEST TOP SIZE CHART

SIZE	1	2	3	4	5	6
BUST	81cm/32"	86.5cm/34"	91.5cm/36"	96.5cm/38"	101.5cm/40"	106.5cm/42"
WAIST	61cm/24"	66cm/26"	71cm/28"	76cm/30"	81cm/32"	86.5cm/34"
HIP	84cm/33"	89cm/35"	94cm/37"	99cm/39"	104cm/41"	109cm/43"

FINISHED GARMENT MEASUREMENTS

The ease of the vest top comes from the natural stretch of the jersey fabric, so the finished garment measurements are the same as above.

Remember to always trace off the pattern and work from the trace copy so that you have the original pattern intact.

- - - - - - - - - - - - - -

TOP TIP FOR NEW PATTERNS

Make a note on the pattern about the new design for your own records. Add the date and draw a little image of the garment so you can always identify it easily.

- - - - - - - - - - - - - -

MAKE THE VEST TOP

YOU WILL NEED

Vest top pattern pieces ◉ Pattern paper ◉ Paper scissors ◉ Tools for transferring marks
Fabric scissors ◉ Pins ◉ Chosen jersey fabric ◉ Matching thread
Single ballpoint needle ◉ Twin ballpoint needles

PREPARE

1 Select the vest top pattern pieces. Trace the size you want to make onto pattern paper and cut out, keeping the original pattern intact.

2 Fold the fabric right sides together, as shown on the fabric layout diagram (see page 70).

3 Place the pattern pieces onto the fabric, aligning the grainlines and making sure each edge marked 'FOLD' is on a fold of the fabric.

4 Pin and cut the fabric pieces.

5 Before taking the pattern pieces off the fabric, transfer all the notches and other markings (see page 17).

ASSEMBLE THE VEST TOP

6 Line up the notches at the shoulder seams and the side seams, and pin.

7 Using the single ballpoint needle and matching thread, set your machine to a narrow zigzag stitch so that it stretches with the movement of the fabric. It's a good idea to sew a sample of zigzag on a spare piece of the jersey

fabric to test the stitch.

8 Sew the shoulder seams and side seams, with the 1.5cm seam allowance included in the pattern. **(A)**

9 If using a fine jersey fabric, trim off the excess to 5mm to avoid a bulky seam.

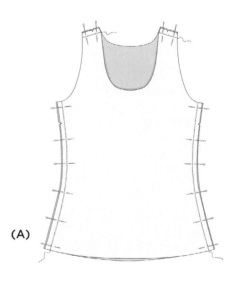

(A)

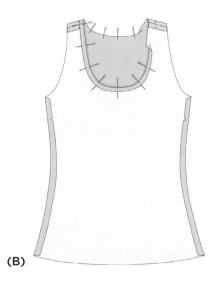

(B)

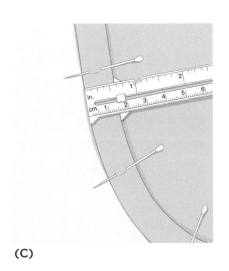

(C)

SEW THE EDGES

10 Change to the twin ballpoint needles and thread them both with matching thread.

11 Set your machine to straight stitch and test it on waste fabric.

12 Start with the neckline, working on the wrong side. Fold the raw edge under by 1.5cm. Pin it in place with the pins at right angles to the edge and the pinheads pointing outwards so you can pull them out at you sew. Use your seam gauge to help keeping your seam allowance equal. **(B & C)**

13 Turn the vest to the right side and, stitch around the neckline,keeping an even distance from the edge and so that the bobbin thread sews over the raw edge, keeping the inside neat. Trim any excess fabric. **(D)**

14 Repeat on both armholes.

15 2.5cm has been allowed for the bottom hem but make the vest top a little shorter if you wish. Turn the hem under and stitch in the same way as for the neckline and armholes.

TOP TIP FOR SAVING THREAD
Wind an additional bobbin with matching thread and use that as your second spool so that you don't need to buy two spools of thread.

- - - - - - - - - - - - -

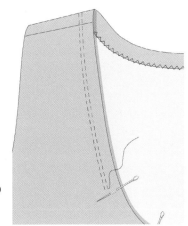

(D)

THE LOUNGE VEST

This relaxed jersey look is achieved by increasing the ease of the vest pattern, opening up the armholes and lowering the neckline slightly.

Your pattern and fabric layout

Use the main vest top pattern as your template for the lounge vest (see page 70). Create your new pattern first to calculate how much fabric you need.

ADAPT THE ORIGINAL PATTERN

1 Trace off your pattern pieces for the vest top onto a new piece of paper. The seam allowances will remain 1.5cm.

2 Starting on the new front pattern, label the centre front line, which won't change.

3 In pencil, draw a parallel line from the side seam, this can be as much or as little as you wish, depending on how much ease you want. We added an extra 4cm to the side seam. This will increase the ease of the vest top.

4 Extend the bottom of the armhole by 2.5cm to meet the new side seamline. Draw a new line for the armhole, copying the original curve of the contours and narrowing up to the strap.

5 Lower the neckline by drawing a new shape, using the original pattern markings as guidelines. We dropped our pattern by 2cm.

6 Draw a new hemline, taking 5cm off the length. **(A)**

7 Assess your new pattern and make any final tweaks.

8 Make the same alterations to the back, leaving the centre back the same. **(B)**

9 Make sure the side seams and straps on both pattern pieces are the same length and width so they fit together.

10 Trace off the new pattern pieces onto a new piece of pattern paper and mark all the relevant notches and markings. Cut out the pattern pieces.

SEW THE LOUNGE VEST

11 To sew this new garment, follow the instructions for the basic vest top (see page 72).

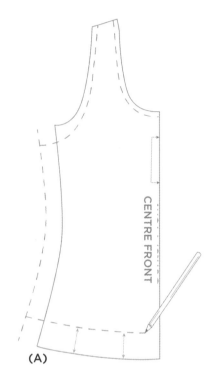

(A)

(B)

Remember to use
your seam gauge
to keep your seam
allowance equal

BECOME A JERSEY SEWING MASTER

Working with jersey can sometimes feel daunting because of the natural stretch in the fabric. However, a domestic sewing machine will stitch jersey perfectly so you won't need to invest in an overlocker. You just need to adjust the settings on your machine. It may take a little practice, and a few samples to get a stitch you are happy with. Twin needles can 'jump' stitches because the needles can't get through the knit or two lines of stitches can cause a tunnelling effect because they are too close together.

Follow these simple tips practising on waste fabric:

- ⬤ **hold the fabric on the machine plate, just firmly enough to allow the fabric to move under the foot**
- ⬤ sew slowly
- ⬤ try lowering the tension
- ⬤ set the presser foot to work with your fabric – too light and it may skip, too heavy and it may pull.

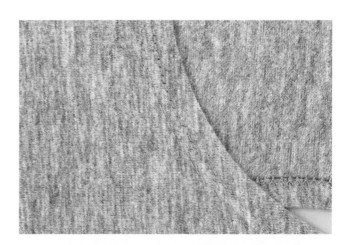

TOP TIP FOR PROTECTING TWIN NEEDLES

Never stitch zigzag with twin needles as they can hit the foot and break.

- - - - - - - - - - - - -

Make it your own

JERSEY DRESS

You can extend the shape of the vest top pattern to make a jersey maxi dress. You can make it close fitting or slightly looser, depending on how much ease you add to the garment.

Before you cut any fabric, we suggest creating your new pattern first, then calculating how much fabric is required. It's also a good idea to make a toile (see page 18) before cutting into your chosen fabric.

1 You need three accurate measurements to adapt the vest top into a dress – for the hip, waist to hip, and waist to hemline. Refer to the chart on page 13 for detailed instructions on how to take these measurements.

2 Trace off your pattern pieces for the vest top onto a new piece of paper long enough to take the whole length of the dress. The shape will change but the seam allowances remain 1.5cm.

3 Extend the centre front line from the waist to your new hemline. Square this off by drawing a 50cm line at right angles to the centre front. This may change and is simply a guideline.

4 Mark your waist to hip measurement on the pattern. Square this off as in step 3. Divide your hip measurement by four, and mark this new measurement from the centre front line. These measurements will make the dress skim your body, if you want some ease here, see page 16 for how to accommodate for this. The jersey will stretch over your shape, but it depends how 'skimmy' you want it to be.

5 Draw a line connecting the waist to your new hipline, making the curve smooth to mimic the shape of your body. Continue the line either straight down to your new hemline or with a little flare. Don't bring the width of the hemline in too much or you won't be able to walk in the dress and you'll only manage tiny steps. You may need to add a side split if that's the case (see page 96).

6 Repeat steps 3–5 for the centre back pattern piece.

7 Make sure the side seams on both pattern pieces are the same length and that you have added 1.5cm seam allowances and a 2.5cm hem allowance.

8 You can lower the neckline, make more or less of the racer back, or make thinner or thicker straps if you wish. Look at the lounge vest for how to do this (see page 74).

9 Trace off the new pattern pieces onto a new piece of pattern paper and mark all the relevant notches and markings. Cut out the pattern pieces.

10 To sew this new garment, follow the instructions for the basic vest top.

LET'S TALK ABOUT EASE

When adapting the vest to a dress, adding just 2.5cm to the width of both pattern pieces will add 10cm to the width of the whole dress.

If you want a super-loose dress, simply draw a line on both pattern pieces straight down from underneath the armhole to the hemline without any waist shaping.

If you draw a wide flare from underarm to hem, you'll create a V-shape that will hang lower at the sides than at the front and back. Experiment, starting with a gentle flare. Then you can adapt the pattern after making a toile. This is where the enjoyment begins in designing your own dress.

TOP TIP FOR MEASURING

For the waist to hemline measurement stand in front of a mirror and hold the tape measure so that zero is where you want the hem. Then you can read off the measurement at your waist, without bending over and getting an inaccurate measurement or get a buddy to help!

- - - - - - - - - - - - -

2

THE SKIRT

IN THIS CHAPTER YOU CAN MAKE:
The skirt (**page 86**)
Sister style: The flared mini
(**page 92**)
A maxi skirt (page 96)
A mullet skirt (page 98)
A wiggle skirt (page 99)

A skirt is essential to any capsule collection. It can reinvent your wardrobe, make a real statement and define your look through all seasons. This pattern has a flattering shape and a classic midi length, skimming below the knee with a barely-there flare, but it can be adjusted easily to any length. We chose to make it from faux leather because there's such a fantastic range of colours and also to tempt you to try working with different materials. We also encourage you to adapt the pattern to make a cute A-line mini. Its flared shape is just as flattering and works cleverly in light linen or heavier wool.

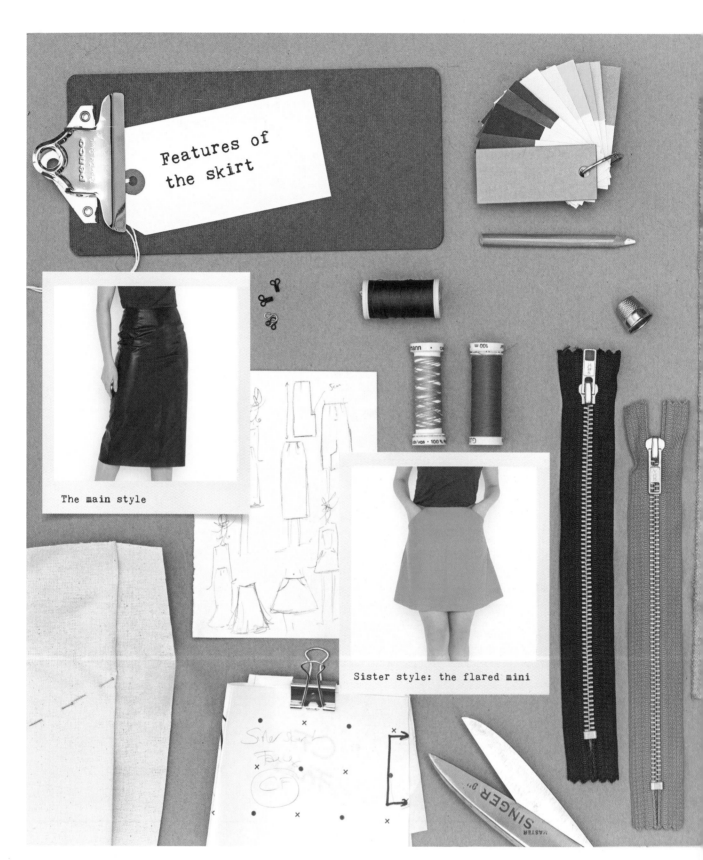

Features of the skirt

The main style

Sister style: the flared mini

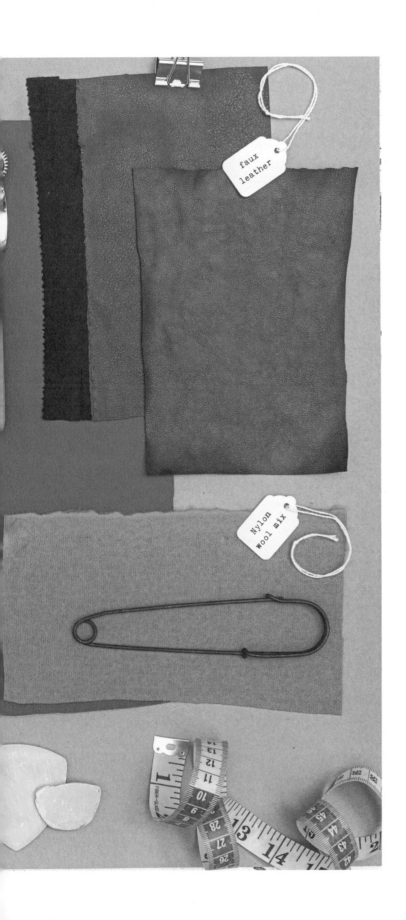

MAIN STYLE

The main skirt is midi
length with a high-rise
waist.
It features:
- a kick pleat
- a concealed zip
- a gentle flare.

SISTER STYLE

The flared skirt is a mini
with a low-rise waist.
It features:
- diagonal pockets
- a concealed zip
- an A-line flare.

SUGGESTED FABRICS

Both skirts work well in
medium- and heavier-weight
fabrics, although using
a lighter material would
work very nicely for a
high summer style. We used
a striking faux leather
in chocolate for the main
skirt and a nylon wool mix
for the sister style.

Your pattern

The skirt has two pattern pieces.

YOU WILL NEED TO CUT:

1 FRONT ON THE FOLD

2 BACKS

A pattern is made separately for the facing, which also needs interfacing. You will have four pattern pieces in total when you have done your facing.

Before you start

Take your measurements (see page 12) and then, if necessary, grade the pattern if you are between sizes (see page 16). We recommend making a toile (see page 18) before making the final garment.

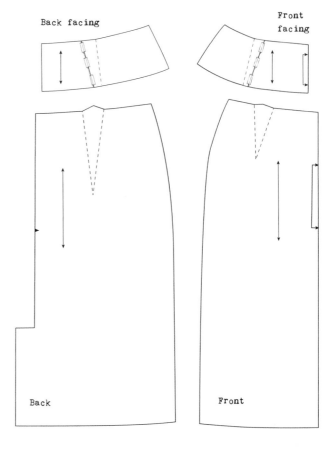

Back facing

Front facing

Back

Front

THE SKIRT SIZE CHART

SIZE	1	2	3	4	5	6
WAIST	61cm/24"	66cm/26"	71cm/28"	76cm/30"	81cm/32"	86.5cm/34"
HIP	84cm/33"	89cm/35"	94cm/37"	99cm/39"	104cm/41"	109cm/43"

FINISHED GARMENT MEASUREMENTS

The ease of the skirt around the waist is 4cm/1½" and 6.5cm/2½" around the hips.

SIZE	1	2	3	4	5	6
WAIST	65cm/25½"	40cm½/27½"	75cm/29½"	81cm/31½"	85cm/33½"	90.5cm/35½"
HIP	90.5cm/35½"	95.5cm/37½"	100.5cm/39½"	105.5cm/41½"	110.5cm/43½"	115.5cm/45½"

Your fabric layout

This layout shows how the pattern pieces can be laid out on the fabric

115cm wide fabric

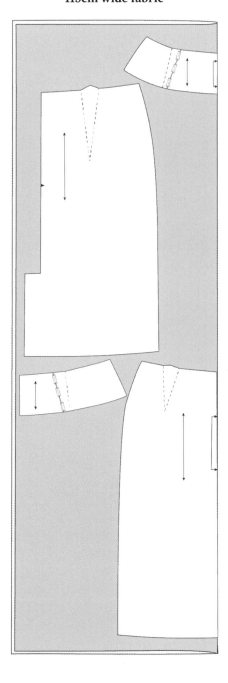

140cm wide fabric

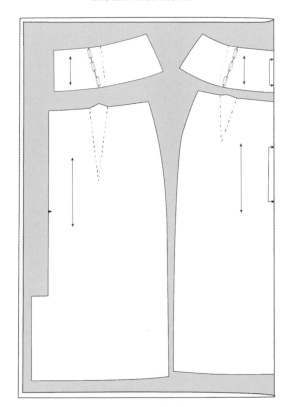

FABRIC QUANTITIES

These quantities include enough fabric for facings.

SIZE	115cm wide	140cm wide
1	181cm/71"	102cm/40"
2	181cm/71"	102cm/40"
3	181cm/71"	102cm/40"
4	181cm/71"	102cm/40"
5	181cm/71"	102cm/40"
6	181cm/71"	102cm/40"

MAKE THE SKIRT

YOU WILL NEED

The skirt pattern pieces ⊗ Pattern paper ⊗ Paper scissors ⊗ Sticky tape ⊗ Tools for transferring marks ⊗ Fabric shears ⊗ Pins ⊗ Fabric weights if using faux leather or leather to help weight the pattern down as pins can cause puncture marks ⊗ Chosen fabric ⊗ Contrast fabric of a similar weight for facings (optional) ⊗ Matching thread ⊗ 0.25m fusible interfacing of a weight to suit the fabric ⊗ 20cm zipper in matching colour ⊗ Hook and eye

PREPARE

1 Select the skirt pattern pieces. Trace the size you want to make onto pattern paper and cut out, keeping the original pattern intact.

2 Before placing your skirt pattern onto your fabric, you'll need to create the facings. To mark out the facings, draw a line across the front and back pattern pieces a consistent distance below the waistline. We chose 10cm, but you could make a deeper facing to avoid it showing through a light-weight fabric. **(A)**

3 Trace the facing pieces onto a separate piece of paper, including the dart markings, grainline and fold placement. Cut out. **(B)**

4 Pinch each pattern together to close the dart, and pin or tape down. This removes the dart from the facings, which will fit your skirt beautifully once you have sewn the darts in the main fabric. You may need to trim a bit of the paper pattern to smooth out the top and bottom curves on the facing pieces. **(C)**

5 When you have all four of your pattern pieces, fold the fabric right sides together, as shown on the fabric layout diagram (see page 85). Place the pattern pieces for the main skirt and facings onto the fabric, aligning the grainlines and making sure the edge marked 'FOLD' is on a fold of the fabric. Pin and cut out the fabric pieces. Before taking the pattern pieces off the fabric, transfer all the notches and other markings (see page 17).

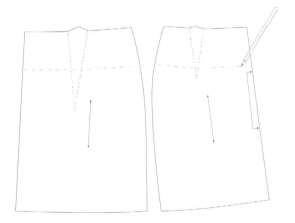

(A)

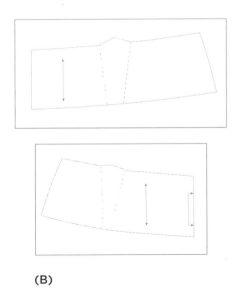

(B)

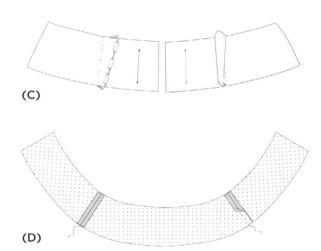

(C)

(D)

6 Place the new facing pattern pieces onto your fabric in the same way. Weight or pin and cut out the fabric. Cut the facing pieces you require from the interfacing following the same pattern guidelines.

ASSEMBLE THE FACING

7 Following the manufacturer's instructions, iron your interfacing on to the relevant facing pieces, then sew the facings together at the side seams, leaving the centre back open. Press the seams open and edge finish the raw edges. **(D)**

SEW THE DARTS

8 Pinch one dart on the main skirt front right sides together. Match up the markings or tailor tacks. Weight or pin to secure the folded fabric together and place another pin at the tip of the dart. Draw a straight guideline from the waistline to the dart point. **(E)**

9 Sew the dart, starting in the seam allowance with a few reverse stitches, and continuing off the fabric at the dart point. Tie a knot in the two threads at the point and trim. This will secure the stitching and give you a nice sharp point. Press to set the stitches, then press the fabric

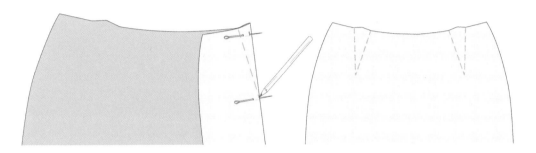

(E)

in the dart towards the side seam. Leather or pleather is difficult to press and to get looking crisp, so use a pressing cloth between your iron and fabric if necessary.

10 Repeat steps 8 and 9 to sew the second dart in the skirt front and then the two darts on the skirt back pieces.

PREPARE THE KICK PLEAT

11 Edge finish the raw edge of the kick pleat with a small hem. Finish 2.5cm before the hem of the skirt. When hemming this will be folded back to create a lovely finish. If you finish the whole edge when doing the hem it could be a little bulky but less fiddly!

12 Fold the raw edges down under the pleat by 5mm, then 5mm again. Press and sew in place. We used pleather, which doesn't fray, so we didn't hem the skirt. We cut it nice and straight so we could finish the kick pleat to the hem.

INSERT THE ZIPPER

13 Insert the invisible zipper, as explained on page 46.

14 Sew the back seam up to your pattern marking just before the beginning of the kick pleat. Reverse stitch to secure.

SEW THE KICK PLEAT

15 Once you have sewn down your back seam to your pattern marking, you need to sew the top of the kick pleat together diagonally. Draw this line in with chalk. The chalk line should drop approximately 4cm from the top of the pleat edge. **(F)**

16 Sew the kick pleat together from your back seam across your diagonal chalk marking. **(G)**

17 Working on the wrong side of the skirt, press the pleat to the right, making sure it is laying flat on the skirt. Pin or sticky tape in place. On

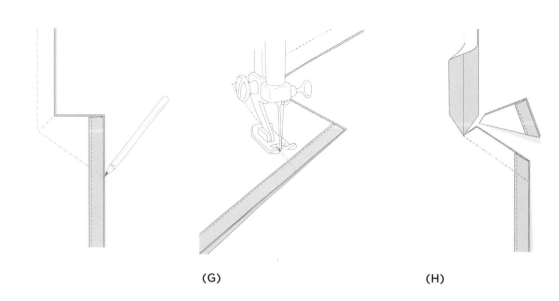

(F) (G) (H)

the right side, make sure the centre back fold on the pleat is perfectly straight.

18 When you're happy with your pleat position, working on the wrong side, sew along your diagonal stitch line, this time sewing the kick pleat to the back of the skirt. This is going to be seen on the outside of the skirt so you want to make it nice and neat.

19 Carefully clip the seam allowance into the pivot point where the pleat meets the back seam and trim off any excess. Butterfly the seams open and edge finish separately or all together, depending on your fabric. **(H)**

20 Working on the right side of your skirt, secure the top of the vent by adding a little bar tack across the top of the pleat. This is two or three stitches where the back seam meets the open pleat. It provides a bit of extra security at the back of the seam. **(I)**

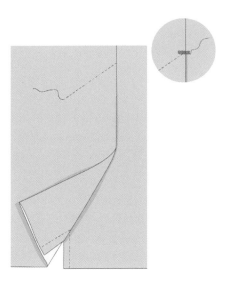

(I)

ADD AN EASY SPLIT

You can easily incorporate a dramatic split in the side or back seam of your skirt. It can be added after you have constructed the skirt but needs to be done before you stitch the hem to ensure you have a neat finish. Take the split high enough to allow you to walk comfortably, but not so high that it reveals too much thigh.

1 Once your skirt has been constructed but before you tackle the hem, mark the top of the split you want with a pin. The seam allowance should be finished and pressed open.

2 Topstitch the seam allowance to the main skirt, 1cm from the seamline. Sewing up one side of the split from the hem, pivot across the top of the split, reverse over the stitch line across the top for reinforcement, then sew down the other side of the split to the hem.

3 Unpick the original seamline to open up the split, then hem the skirt as usual.

ASSEMBLE THE SKIRT

21 Sticky tape or pin the skirt front and back pieces right sides together. Sew down both side seams matching all notches. Press the seams open and finish the raw edges.

22 Turn the skirt right sides out and open the zipper.

23 Sticky tape or pin the facing to the skirt, right sides together, matching the side seams and waistline edge. Make sure the seam allowances on the side seams lay open, but that the seam allowances on the centre back are folded under. Sew the facing to the skirt. **(J)**

24 Press the seam allowance towards the facing. Reduce any bulk, depending on the weight of your fabric, by layering the seam allowance so that the facing lies flat. (See page 60.) **(K)**

25 Understitch the seam allowance to the facing and press. Then tuck the seam allowance at the centre back under the facing so that it lies smoothly against the zipper and slip stitch in place. **(L)**

26 Pop a few hand stitches by the side seams to keep the facing in place. Sew a hook and eye (see page 55) to the facing to secure the centre back above the zipper.

FINISH WITH A HEM

27 We used pleather, which doesn't fray, so we didn't hem the skirt. If you use a different fabric that requires hemming turn under 5mm along the bottom raw edge and press. Turn under another 2cm and press.

28 Depending on your fabric, hand stitch or machine finish the hem (see pages 44 and 45).

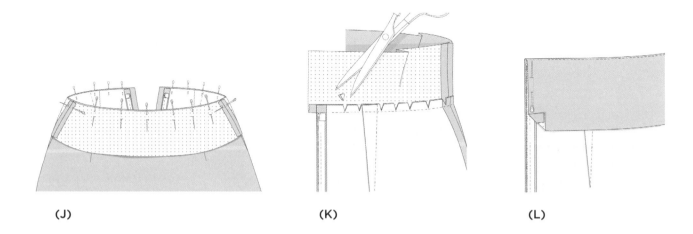

(J) (K) (L)

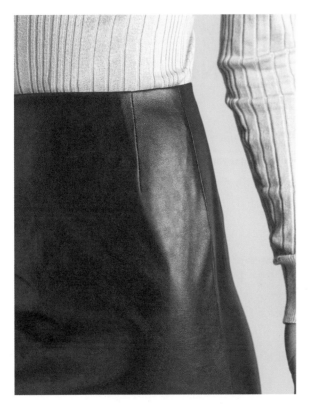

TOP TIPS FOR SEWING WITH FAUX LEATHER

If using faux leather or similar, sticky tape fabric in place, this prevents the pins marking and puncturing the 'skin'.

There's no need to edge finish or hem faux leather as it doesn't fray.

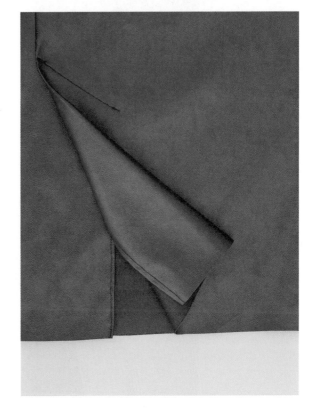

THE FLARED MINI

Our alternative look is a light summer mini skirt. It's shorter in length, sits on the hips, flares out gently in an A-line and has cute diagonal pockets.

Your fabric layout

This layout shows how the pattern pieces can be laid out on the fabric.

115cm wide fabric

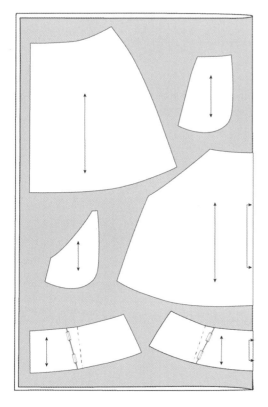

140cm wide fabric

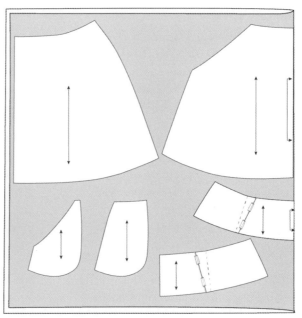

YOU WILL NEED

You will need the same tools and materials as for the original pattern.

PATTERN KNOWHOW

To adapt the pattern to create the flair we used the Slash Method which cuts and spreads open the pattern to increase the volume.

- - - - - - - - - - - - -

FABRIC QUANTITIES

These quantities include enough fabric for facings.

SIZE	115cm wide	140cm wide
1	120cm/47"	120cm/47"
2	120cm/47"	120cm/47"
3	120cm/47"	120cm/47"
4	140cm/55"	140cm/55"
5	140cm/55"	140cm/55"
6	140cm/55"	140cm/55"

ADAPT THE PATTERN

1 Trace off your pattern pieces for the skirt onto a new piece of paper. The shape will change but the seam allowances will remain 1.5cm.

2 Decide where you want the top of the skirt to sit and make a note of how far this is below your waistline. We dropped the waistline by 2.5cm. Mark the new waistline on the pattern pieces, remembering to include a seam allowance. Drawing in the SA around the edge of your pattern first helps give more of an idea of where the skirt will sit and then make any changes from the stitching line not from the cut edge line. Just remember to add in seam allowance on your new dropped waist line. Don't worry about drawing through the darts, we'll be getting rid of them in the next few steps.

3 Decide on the length of the new skirt. Mark this on the pattern pieces, measuring from the new waistline and remembering to account for the seam and hem allowances.

4 On the front pattern piece, draw a vertical line, parallel to the centre front, from the end point of the dart to the new hem. Repeat on the back piece.

5 Cut the pattern pieces out.

6 On each pattern piece, cut along the parallel line to the dart, then along the right-hand dart line. Each pattern piece is now split into two. **(A)**

7 Tape the two pieces for the skirt front together, joining them along the uncut dart line. This will make the pattern flare out below the dart. Repeat with the skirt back. Check that the amount of flair on the front and back pieces is the same. **(B)**

8 Trace off the new pattern pieces onto a new piece of pattern paper, incorporating the flare, to give you a new A-line pattern. Make sure the side seams on both patterns are the same length. **(C)**

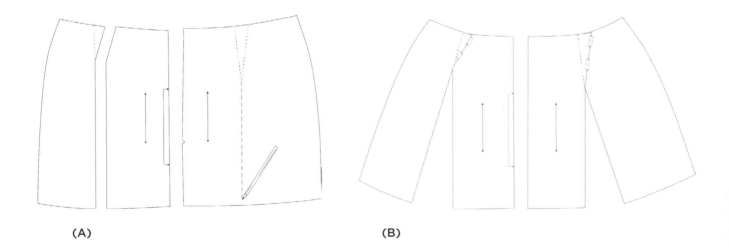

(A)

(B)

9 Prepare pattern pieces for the facing in the same way as for the original skirt.

10 Adapt the pattern to incorporate diagonal pockets, as explained on page 62. **(D)**

11 Before cutting out the new pattern pieces, transfer all the relevant notches and other markings.

ASSEMBLE THE SKIRT

12 Cut out all the pattern pieces. Make sure you transfer all the relevant notches, foldlines and other markings from the original pattern. Use the pattern pieces to cut out the fabric.

13 Sew the pockets in place on the pieces for the skirt front, following the instructions on page 62.

14 Join the two skirt back pieces together and insert the concealed zipper, as explained on page 48.

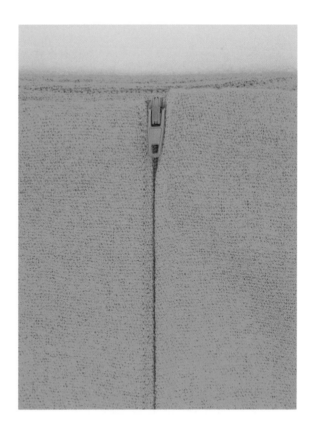

15 Sew the facings together and assemble the skirt as for the original design. Hem.

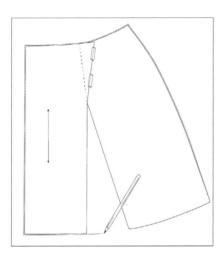

(C)

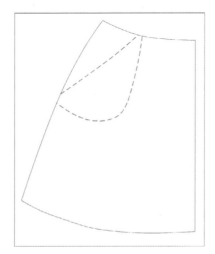

(D)

Make it your own
MAXI SKIRT

Maxi skirts are a wardrobe staple for most of us in the summer months. They're cool, comfortable and easy to style.

This style, adapted from the main skirt pattern, drapes to the ankle and has two long side splits to create that floaty summer skirt. If you want the skirt to sit lower than the waist, follow the instructions for the flared mini. Otherwise work directly with the main skirt pattern. Alternatively incorporate the flared mini instructions for a floaty maxi skirt.

1 Trace off your pattern pieces for the front and back skirt onto a new piece of paper. Cut them out. You won't need the kick pleat extension, so even off the back seam so it is straight.

2 Cut across the lengthen/shorten lines on each pattern piece and place them on a new piece of paper long enough to incorporate the maxi length. Extend the pattern pieces to your desired length. Pin or tape them to the new piece of paper.

3 Redraw the side seams, keeping lines smooth.

4 Trace off the new pattern pieces onto a new piece of pattern paper, if you wish. Mark all the notches and markings.

5 Mark where you want the splits in the side seams to finish. You could put a split in one or both sides. Make sure your marks match on the front and the back pieces.

6 Cut out the fabric and transfer the notches and other markings.

7 Construct the skirt in the usual way. If you are planning to have in-seam pockets (see page 61), inset them before sewing the side seams. When you get to the side seams, sew down the seam to the notch for the slit, then reverse stitch for 1cm. Set the machine for a longer, tacking (basting) stitch and sew the rest of the seam to the hem.

8 Press the side seams open and finish the raw edges.

9 Starting at the hem and sewing parallel to the seamline, topstitch the seam allowance to the main fabric, up to the top of the split, across the seamline and back down the other side.

10 Remove the basting (tacking) stitches to open up each split.

11 Hem and you'll have your floaty summer maxi skirt!

Make it your own
MULLET SKIRT

Also known as high-low or waterfall skirts, the mullet has a hem that is higher
at the front and lower at the back.

1 Trace off your pattern pieces for the front and back skirt onto a new piece of paper. Cut them out and place them on another piece of paper long enough to incorporate the new skirt length. Again the kick pleat extension isn't needed.

2 Mark the length you want the skirt to be at the front on the centre front foldline. Mark the length you want the skirt to be at the sides on the front side seam. Draw in a soft curve from the side seam to the centre front.

3 Mark the side seam on the skirt back pattern to match the side seam on the front pattern.

4 Repeat step 2 to mark the full length of the mullet on the centre back seam and the curve to the side seam.

5 You should have a smooth curve that starts higher at the front and drops down at the back. Once you are happy with the shape, trace off the pattern onto a new piece of pattern paper and transfer all the notches and markings.

6 Make up the skirt following the main skirt instructions.

Make it your own
WIGGLE SKIRT

Channel your inner Marilyn Monroe by making your own 1950s wiggle skirt. It sits on the waist and makes you wiggle as you walk because the hem is narrower than the hips.

1 Trace off your pattern pieces for the main skirt onto a new piece of paper.

2 On the base pattern, the total amount of ease for the hips is 6.5cm. If you want a tighter fit around the hips, reduce the ease and keep the reduction on the side seams even at hip level. (See page 16 for ease guidelines.)

3 Decide how wide you want the skirt to be at the hem. To get an idea take a step and place a tape measure around the circumference of where you want your skirt hem to be. Divide this by four and that will give you an idea on skirt circumference. A kick pleat or a small split at the back will help you to wiggle more easily without ripping the back seam and won't interfere with the shape of the skirt. Mark the pattern pieces at the side seams to cater for the narrow hemline.

4 Draw a straight line joining the marks at the hip and the hemline matching the front and back pattern pieces.

5 Trace off the new pattern pieces onto a new piece of pattern paper, if you wish, and mark all the relevant notches and markings. Cut out the fabric and make up the skirt following the main skirt instructions.

THE SHIFT DRESS

IN THIS CHAPTER YOU CAN MAKE:
The shift dress (**page 106**)
Sister Style: The tent shift (**page 110**)
Different necklines, collars and sleeves
(**pages 116, 118 and 120**)

A capsule wardrobe wouldn't be complete without a dress and this shift dress earns its place in our collection because it cleverly marries simplicity and versatility. There's no denying the shift dress is a classic, yet it can be quietly understated with straightforward lines and modest length or it can be confidently playful with a mischievous A-line and micro mini-ness. Our design sits nicely between the two. It can certainly have a courtly appearance if you make it in a heavy cotton or rich wool blend but, by raising the hem and adding delicate capped sleeves, you'll transform the more elegant shape into a bolder, sexier mini-shift. Our sister style is a beautiful tent shift that will float and drape effortlessly when made from lighter cotton or silk, allowing full freedom of movement – ideal for summer strolling or evening lounging.

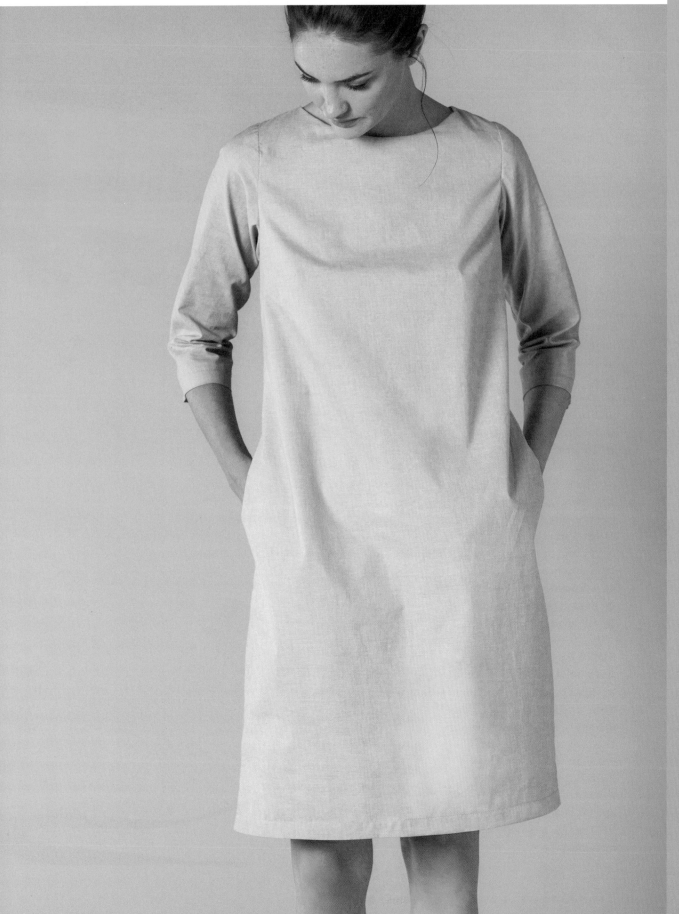

Features of
the shift dress

MAIN STYLE

The shift dress is semi-
fitted with an above the
knee hemline.
It features:

- a round neckline
- three-quarter length
  sleeves
- an invisible zipper
- in-seam pockets.

SISTER STYLE

The sister make is a
sleeveless, oversized
'tent' style shift with
calfline hemline.
It features:

- a round neckline
- over the head access
- in-seam pockets.

SUGGESTED FABRICS

This shift dress works well
with all woven fabrics. We
made the main shift using
a grey cotton chambray and
the sister style using a
silk in black charcoal.
Both light-weight and
heavier cottons work well
and a thicker wool blend
will make a gorgeous
autumnal look.

The shift dress

Sister style: The tent shift

Silk

Black

Cotton poplin

Navy

Rose

Heavy-weight cotton

Cotton chambray

Light grey

Your pattern

The shift dress has six pattern pieces

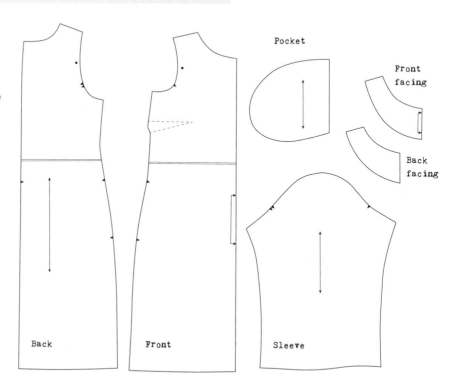

YOU WILL NEED TO CUT:
1 FRONT ON THE FOLD
2 BACKS
1 FRONT FACING ON THE FOLD
+ 1 FROM INTERFACING
2 BACK FACINGS
+ 2 FROM INTERFACING
2 SLEEVES
4 POCKETS

Before you start

Take your measurements (see page 12) and then, if necessary, grade the pattern if you are between sizes (see page 16). We recommend making a toile before making the final garment (see page 18).

THE SHIFT DRESS SIZE CHART

SIZE	1	2	3	4	5	6
BUST	81cm/32"	86.5cm/34"	91.5cm/36"	96.5cm/38"	101.5cm/40"	106.5cm/42"
WAIST	61cm/24"	66cm/26"	71cm/28"	76cm/30"	81cm/32"	86.5cm/34"
HIP	84cm/33"	89cm/35"	94cm/37"	99cm/39"	104cm/41"	109cm/43"

FINISHED GARMENT MEASUREMENTS

The ease of the dress is 7.5cm/3" around the bust, 28cm/11" around the waist and 18cm/7" around the hips.

SIZE	1	2	3	4	5	6
BUST	88.5cm/35"	94cm/37"	99cm/39"	104cm/41"	109cm/43"	114cm/45"
WAIST	89cm/35"	94cm/37"	95cm/39"	104cm/41"	109cm/43"	114.5cm/45"
HIP	102cm/40"	107cm/42"	112cm/44"	117cm/46"	122cm/48"	127cm/50"

Your fabric layout

This layout shows how the pattern pieces can be laid out on the fabric.

115cm wide fabric

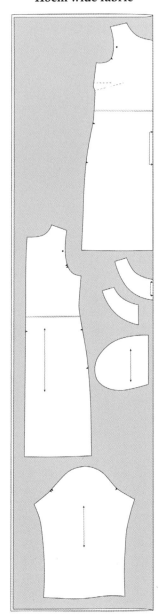

140cm wide fabric

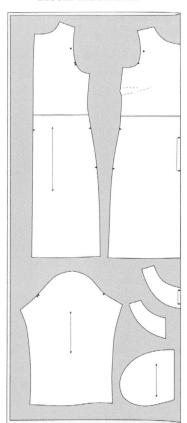

Remember to always trace off the pattern and work from the trace copy so that you have the original pattern intact.

FABRIC QUANTITIES

These quantities include enough fabric for facings.

SIZE	115cm wide	140cm wide
1	262cm/103"	163cm/64"
2	262cm/103"	163cm/64"
3	262cm/103"	163cm/64"
4	268cm/105½"	167cm/65½"
5	268cm/105½"	167cm/65½"
6	268cm/105½"	167cm/65½"

MAKE THE DRESS

YOU WILL NEED

The shift dress pattern pieces ⊗ Pattern paper ⊗ Paper scissors ⊗ Sticky tape
Tools for transferring marks ⊗ Fabric shears ⊗ Pins ⊗ Chosen fabric
Contract fabric of a similar weight for facings (optional) ⊗ Matching thread ⊗ 40cm length invisible zipper
0.25m fusible interfacing, weight to suit fabric ⊗ Hook and eye

PREPARE

1 Select the shift dress pattern pieces. Trace the size you want to make onto pattern paper and cut out, keeping the original pattern intact.

2 Fold the fabric right sides together, as shown on the fabric layout diagram (see page 105) and place the paper patterns onto the fabric, aligning the grainlines and making sure each edge marked 'FOLD' is on a fold of the fabric.

3 Pin and cut out the fabric pieces. Before taking the pattern pieces off the fabric, transfer all the markings (see page 17).

4 Cut the pieces you require from the interfacing.

SEW THE BUST DARTS

5 Sew the bust darts into the dress front fabric as explained on page 22. Then press the darts down towards the hem of the dress. **(A)**

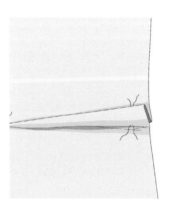

(A)

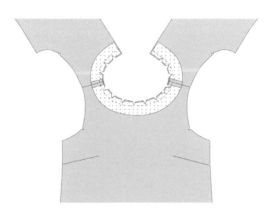

(B)

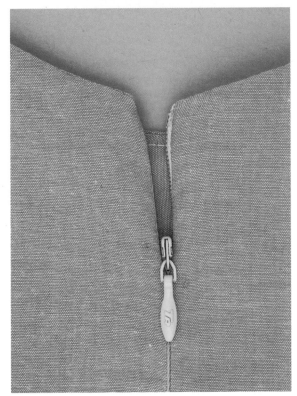

CONSTRUCT THE NECKLINE

6 Place the front and back pieces right sides together, matching the notches at the shoulder seams. Sew the shoulder seams. Press the seams open.

7 Fuse the interfacing to the facing pieces and sew the front and back facings right sides together at the shoulder seams, matching the notches. Press the seams open.

8 Pin the facing around the neckline of the main garment, matching the shoulder seams. (If you are planning to insert a collar, this is where you would insert it.) Sew all around the neckline from centre back to centre back to attach the facing.

9 Clip into the seam allowance to allow the neckline to sit nicely. Press and edge finish the raw edges. Flip the facing inside the dress and press again. **(B, page 106)**

10 Understitch the facing to the seam allowance to prevent it inching out over the neckline. Secure the outer edges of the facing to each shoulder seam with a couple of stitches.

ADD THE POCKETS

11 Attach the in-seam pockets to the front and back pieces as explained on page 61. **(C)**

ASSEMBLE THE DRESS

12 Pin the front and back right sides together along the side seams and around the pockets, matching the notches.

13 Sew the side seams from under the arms to the hem, dealing with the pockets as explained for in-seam pockets on page 61.

14 Finish the raw edges to prevent fraying.

INSERT THE SLEEVES

15 Pin the underarm seam on each sleeve right sides together, matching the notches. Press each seam open and finish the raw edges.

16 Using either a long stitch on the machine or a hand stitch, sew two parallel lines of tacking (basting) in the seam allowance around each sleeve head from one notch to the other. **(D)** The first line of stitches should be 5mm from the edge, the second 2mm from the edge. Keep the thread ends loose on the wrong side of the fabric to make gathering easier. Two lines of tacking

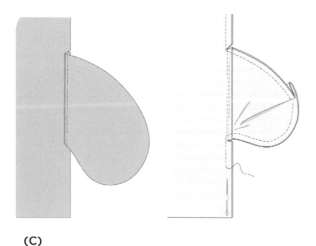

(C)

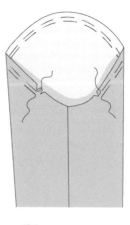

(D)

helps to ease the sleeve neatly into the armhole.

17 Working on one sleeve, gently pull the loose ends of the two threads so that the sleeve head gathers. Although it looks like the fabric will pucker, with a little patience it won't when inserted into the armhole. **(E)**

18 With the sleeve right side out, pin the side seam of the dress to the seam on the sleeve, right sides together. Continue pinning the pieces together around the armhole seam, up to the notches.

19 Match the tailor tack for the centre of the sleeve head with the shoulder seam and pin right sides together.

20 Ease the sleeve head around the armhole so that the gathers are evenly distributed and pin right sides together matching tailor tacks.

21 Tack (baste) the sleeve in place. Turn right sides out and check that the sleeve head sits smoothly in the armhole. Once you are happy with its appearance on the right side,

sew it in place.

22 Press just the seam allowance to flatten any fullness. Finish the raw edges and repeat steps 17–22 on the other sleeve.

23 For each sleeve hem, turn under 5mm, then 2cm. Press, then sew the hem in place with an invisible stitch or top-stitch.

INSERT AN INVISIBLE ZIPPER

24 Insert an invisible zipper into the dress back as explained on page 46. **(F)**

25 Fold the facing back to the wrong side of the dress over the top of the zipper tape. Fold the edges under so they don't interfere with the zipper and pin. Secure the facing ends to the zipper tape with a few hand stitches.

HEM THE DRESS

26 For the hem of the dress, turn under 5mm, then 2cm. Press, then topstitch or hand stitch the hem in place.

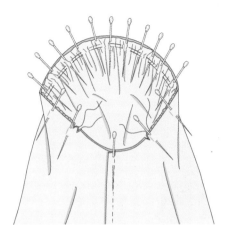

(E)

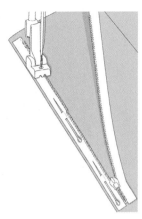

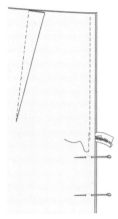

(F)

Sister style
THE TENT SHIFT

This oversized shift is more informal and opens out to a gorgeous billowing shape, which works wonderfully well with lighter, softer fabrics.

Your fabric layout

This layout shows how the pattern pieces can be laid out on the fabric.

115cm wide fabric

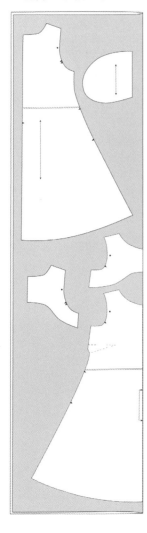

140cm wide fabric

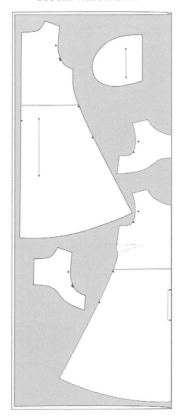

YOU WILL NEED

The zip and sleeve pattern pieces aren't needed for this make. The rest of the tools are the same as the main pattern.

TOP TIP FOR A GOOD FIT

We recommend making a toile (see page 18) before making the garment.

- - - - - - - - - - - - -

FABRIC QUANTITIES

These quantities include enough fabric for facings.

SIZE	115cm wide	140cm wide
1	260cm/102½"	260cm/102½"
2	260cm/102½"	260cm/102½"
3	260cm/102½"	260cm/102½"
4	260cm/102½"	260cm/102½"
5	260cm/102½"	260cm/102½"
6	260cm/102½"	260cm/102½"

ADAPT THE PATTERN

1 Trace off your pattern piece for the shift dress front onto a new sheet of paper. The shape will change but the seam allowances will remain 1.5cm.

2 On the new pattern piece, extend the pattern if you want a longer length (we extended ours by 10cm) then draw in a new front neckline and armhole keeping the lines smooth. As there is no zipper you want to make sure that this neck hole fits over your head, this can be a bit of trial and error and can be adapted in the toile. If you are using lightweight fabric such as silk or cotton lawn, you can make narrow shoulder straps. If using a wool or chunkier/stiffer fabric, you'll need wider straps as the fabric needs to be pulled through the shoulder seams. **(A)**

3 Place another piece of pattern paper over the neckline and armhole. Trace off one facing to incorporate the neckline and the armhole, following the seamlines very carefully. The bottom edge of the facing should start just above the dart at the side seam and rise in a gentle curve to the centre front.

4 Now adapt the width of the dress front. Working from the hemline, make three evenly spaced cuts up to the waistline, giving you four even strips of pattern paper to work with and cut up these lines to the waistline. **(B)**

5 Place this pattern onto a new sheet of pattern paper large enough for a wide tent-style dress. Sticky tape around the top of the dress to the waistline and down the centre front, keeping the centre front in its original straight line.

6 Fan out the cut strips, extending the dress

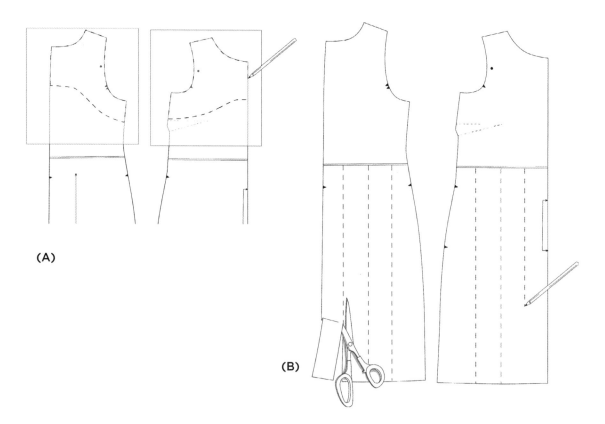

(A)

(B)

to the side. Make mini creases at the top of the strips to help them fan out. Sticky tape these in place. **(C)**

7 From the centre front, create a soft new curve matching up to the side seam on the hem. Make sure they are an equal length. From the bust dart soften the curve to meet the new side seam. **(D)** Extend the centre front and side seam by the same measurement to create the new length.

8 When you are happy with the shape, sticky tape in place.

9 Repeat steps 1–8 for the dress back, making sure the width and length of the back match the front, pinching together the dart on the front to take that into account so the length is even . Also make sure the new shapings on the front

and back match at the shoulders and at the top of the side seam.

10 When you are happy with the shape of your dress, trace around each pattern piece onto the pattern paper underneath, remembering to include seam/hem allowances if applicable. Transfer side seam and shoulder seam notches from the original pattern. Cut out the new pattern pieces.

11 Check your notches and pocket placements match up on both pattern pieces. Adjust these notches if necessary so that they match up on your fabric.

12 Place your new pattern pieces on the dress fabric, making sure the dress front and the front facing are on a fold. Pin and cut out.

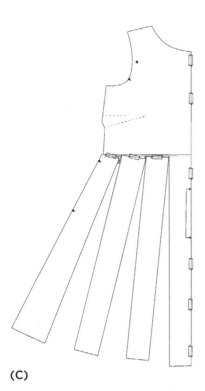

(C)

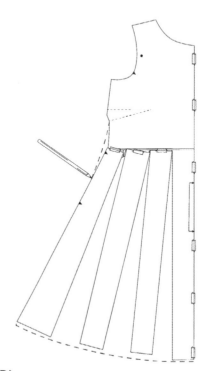

(D)

SEW THE DARTS

13 Sew the bust darts into the dress front as explained on page 22. Press the darts down towards the hem of the dress

ATTACHING THE FACING

14 Place the front and the back pieces right sides together, matching up the notches at the shoulder seams. Pin and sew the shoulder seams. Press the seams open.

15 Fuse the interfacing to the facing pieces. Sew the front and back facings together at the shoulder seams, matching the notches. Press open. Edge finish the raw edges along the bottom edges of the facing.

16 Pin the facing to the front and back pieces, right sides together, matching the shoulder seams. Sew around the neckline from centre back to centre back. Sew around each armhole from side seam to side seam.

17 Clip into the seam allowances around the inner curves of the neckline and armholes so the facing will sit neatly. Press. **(E)**

18 Turn right sides out by pulling each back piece though the shoulder strap. Press the facing neatly in place. **(F)**

19 Understitch the facing at the neckline and underarm to the seam allowance to prevent it inching over the top of the dress. You won't be able to access all areas but do as much as you can. Press.

ADD THE POCKETS

20 Attach the in-seam pockets to the front and back pieces as explained on page 61.

COMPLETE THE DRESS

21 Pin the front and back right sides together, from the facings under the armholes, along the side seams and around the pockets down to the hem, matching the notches.

22 Sew the side seams from the facing to the hem, dealing with the pockets as explained for in-seam pockets on page 61. Finish the raw edges to prevent fraying.

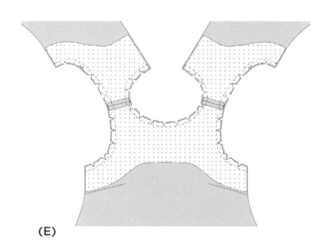

(E)

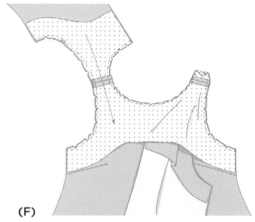

(F)

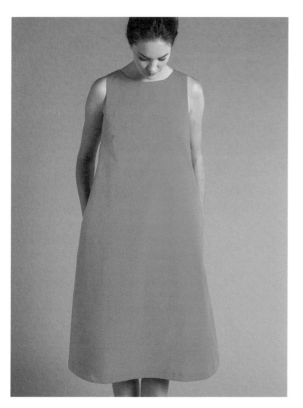

23 Pin the back pieces right sides together along the back seam, starting with the facing and going all the way down to the hem. Sew in place. Press and then finish the raw edges.

24 Finally, hem the dress. The hemline is on a slight curve so the dress will require either a tiny rolled hem or a wider hem that may have tiny pleats when folded. Press these flat to reduce bulk. For hemming options, turn to page 44. Press.

CHOOSE YOUR NECKLINE

You could adapt the shift dress to give it a twist with a different neckline.
Here are six of our favourites for you to choose from. Different necklines require
different layering tecniques to help them lie flat. See page 60 for options.

CLOSE NECK

This close round neck is perfect for
adding a Peter Pan or pointed flat
collar. Or left unadorned, it will look
pleasingly understated.

SQUARE NECK

Cutting right across the chest, the
square neck creates a wider look to the
upper body. It works best on narrow
shoulders.

SCOOP NECK

A scoop is wider and lower than a
round neck and its open style reveals
the neck and collar.

SLASH NECK

The slash neck is a confident choice, uncovering the neck and shoulders. It works well with long sleeves.

V-NECK

The deeper the V, the more it highlights the neck and bust. The Chelsea collar works well on this neckline shape.

SWEETHEART NECK

The gentle curve of this sweetheart variation enhances the bust, creating a flatteringly shape.

HOW TO ALTER THE NECKLINE

1 Trace off your pattern pieces for the original shift dress front onto a new piece of pattern paper.

2 Sketch your chosen neckline onto the new front pattern. Check you are happy with the shape and style. When you are happy, add a seam allowance.

3 If you want a facing, rather than using bias binding (see page 42), place another piece of pattern paper over the neckline. Trace off a facing, following the neckline very carefully. The facing should be about 7cm deep. See our tent dress on page 112.

4 Repeat steps 1–3 to adapt the back pattern piece too if you wish, making sure that it matches the front pattern at the shoulders.

5 Cut out the new pattern pieces.

Make it your own

CHOOSE YOUR COLLAR

We have included pattern pieces for three different collars on the pattern sheets. They all fit the shift dress and blouse designs in this book and they can all be attached in the same way.

HOW TO ATTACH A COLLAR

A collar has two parts, each with a top and a facing. They meet at the centre front and the centre back of the garment, and are attached by sandwiching them between the main garment and the garment facing.

1 Trace off your chosen collar pattern and make a toile of a single layer of calico to get the perfect shape. Make sure the inside measurement of the collar matches the neckline of the garment.

2 When you are happy with the collar shape, use it as your pattern and cut two pairs of collars from your fabric. You'll have four collar pieces – a top and a facing for the right and another pair for the left.

3 Cut a pair of collar shapes from lightweight fusible interfacing. Fuse the interfacing to each of the collar facing pieces.

4 Pin the top and facing for one collar piece right sides together. Sew across one short edge, along the longest edge of the collar and across the other short edge, leaving the neck edge open. Clip across the seam allowance around the curves and trim excess fabric from any points, corners and seams, which will help the collar to sit flat and the shape to look clean. Press.

5 Turn the collar right sides out. Carefully poke out any corners and points. Press.

6 Staystitch through all the layers around the open raw edge to help stabilise the curve.

7 Repeat steps 4–6 for the other collar piece.

8 Working on the right side of the garment, pin both collar pieces in place, starting at the centre front to make sure that they sit perfectly on the centre front of the garment. Pin them around the neckline, making sure they sit perfectly at the centre back.

9 Make the facing and attach it to the garment as in steps 6–10 for the main shift dress, sandwiching the collar in place. The seam allowance may need grading to reduce the bulk of multiple layers of fabric (see page 60).

10 When you have understitched the facing in place, the collar will sit beautifully flat around the neckline.

POINTED FLAT COLLAR
The flat collar has sharper edges for
a smarter finish and sits flat to the
décolletage.

PETER PAN COLLAR
A Peter Pan collar, which sits close to
the neck on a round curve, has feminine
charm and bookish appeal.

CHELSEA COLLAR
The Chelsea collar works with a
V-neckline or low scoop. It creates a
statement with its long, exaggerated line.

Make it your own

CHOOSE YOUR SLEEVES

Deciding on the best sleeve shape is a balance between the fabric choice, your body shape and the length and fit of the garment. The shift dress pattern has three-quarter-length fitted sleeves and we love the simplicity of the shape as it flatters the upper arms and works well in both heavier and lighter fabrics. However, if you want to try something different, here are three other options.

HOW TO MAKE THE LONG SLEEVES WITH SPLIT CUFF

1 Measure around your wrist and around your bent elbow, making sure that you include ease. Measure your arm for the length of the new sleeve. Make a note.

2 Trace off your pattern for the shift dress sleeve onto a new piece of pattern paper. Mark the length of the new sleeve onto your pattern. Draw in the new hemline and add a hem allowance of 2.5cm.

3 Draw new underarm seamlines to create the shape of the new sleeve, starting at the top of the original seamline and extending the line to the new width at the hem. Mark how deep you want the split on this line. Transfer relevant notches and markings from the original pattern, then cut out your new sleeve pattern.

4 Sew the underarm seam right sides together down to the split detail and backstitch. Press, keeping the seamline turned under along the split. Finish the raw edges. Hem the bottom edge of the sleeve, making sure that the corners of the split are level and crisp. Press.

5 Topstitch around the hem, then continue around the split about 1cm from the seamline.

HOW TO MAKE THE BELL SLEEVES

1 Decide how long you want the sleeve and how wide you want the bell shape to be. Make a note of the measurements.

2 Trace off your pattern for the shift dress sleeve onto a new piece of pattern paper large enough for the new shape.

3 Mark the length of the new sleeve onto your pattern. Draw in the new hemline and add a hem allowance of 2.5cm.

4 Draw new underarm seamlines to create the bell shape of the new sleeve. If you want the sleeve to flare the full length, start from the top of the original seamline, extending your line to the new width at the hem. If you want the sleeve to flare from the elbow or elsewhere, start your new line from that point.

5 Transfer relevant notches and markings from the original pattern, then cut out your new sleeve pattern.

HOW TO MAKE THE CAP SLEEVES

1 Trace off your pattern for the shift dress sleeve onto a new piece of pattern paper.

2 Measure from the top of your shoulder to find the right length for your cap sleeve. Cap sleeves generally finish 2.5–5cm below the shoulder seam

3 Mark this measurement onto your new pattern, starting from the seamline at the sleeve head. Add a hem allowance of 2.5cm. Using a ruler, draw a horizontal line through the mark and across the sleeve pattern.

4 Transfer relevant notches and markings from the original pattern, then cut out your new sleeve pattern.

4

THE TROUSERS

IN THIS CHAPTER YOU CAN MAKE:
The trousers **(page 128)**
Sister Style: The high and wide trousers **(page 133)**
Trouser turn-ups **(page 138)**
Skinnier legs (page 140)
Culottes **page (page 142)**

Trousers are a wardrobe staple and there are many features to consider when making them, including the shape, length and rise. We chose a straight leg trouser, to give an effortlessly elegant silhouette. It's a shape that will look great wherever you want the waistline and hem to sit. If you prefer a wider leg, the sister style gives you that more relaxed cut. Trousers are often seen as the most challenging of projects but, if you get accurate measurements, you'll get a great fit – and getting a great fit will make you feel like a better version of you!

The trousers

Features of
the trousers

Sister style: High and wide

Cotton
needle
cord

Wool
cashmere
blend

Light
mint

Burgundy

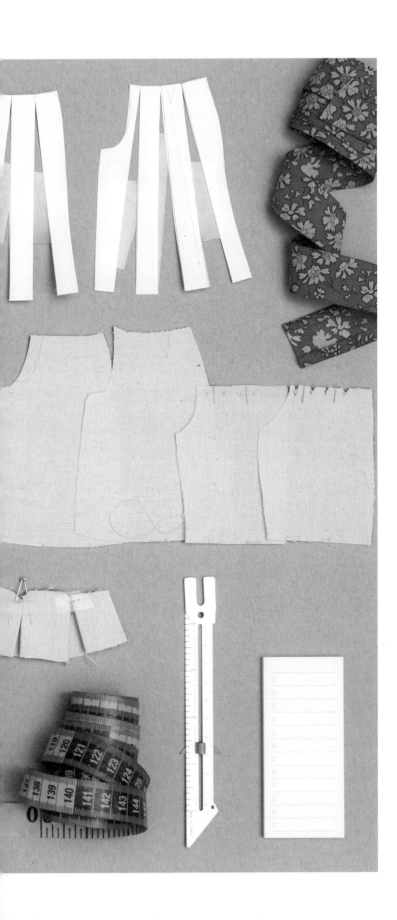

MAIN STYLE

The main trousers are fitted with a mid-rise waist.
They feature:
- a straight leg
- front fly fastening
- diagonal pockets
- single welt pocket.

SISTER STYLE

A looser fit with front fly fastening.
It features:
- a wide leg
- a high waist.

SUGGESTED FABRICS

These trousers work well in all woven fabrics from wool to lightweight cotton.
We used a burgundy cotton needle cord (corduroy) for the main trousers and a cashmere wool blend in mint for the sister trousers.

Your pattern

The trousers have eight pattern pieces.

YOU WILL NEED TO CUT:

2 FRONTS
2 BACKS
2 DIAGONAL POCKETS PIECES
2 DIAGONAL POCKET LININGS
2 WAISTBANDS + 1 FROM INTERFACING.
5 BELT LOOPS AND A FLY GUARD.
WELT POCKET PIECE

Before you start

Take your measurements (see page 12) and then, if necessary, grade the pattern if you are between sizes (see page 16). We recommend making a toile before making the final garment (see page 18).

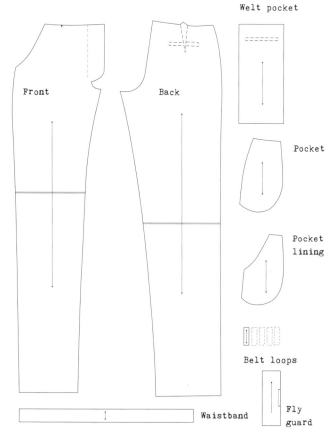

THE TROUSERS SIZE CHART

SIZE	1	2	3	4	5	6
WAIST	61cm/24"	66cm/26"	71cm/28"	76cm/30"	81cm/32"	86.5cm/34"
HIP	84cm/33"	89cm/35"	94cm/37"	99cm/39"	104cm/41"	109cm/43"

FINISHED GARMENT MEASUREMENTS
The ease of the trousers around the waist is 4cm/1½" and 6.5cm/2½" around the hips.

SIZE	1	2	3	4	5	6
WAIST	65cm/25½"	40cm½/27½"	75cm/29½"	81cm/31½"	85cm/33½"	90.5cm/35½"
HIP	90.5cm/35½"	95.5cm/37½"	100.5cm/39½"	105.5cm/41½"	110.5cm/43½"	115.5cm/45½"

Your fabric layout

This layout shows how the pattern pieces can be laid out on the fabric.

115cm wide fabric

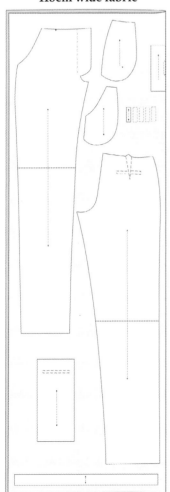

140cm wide fabric

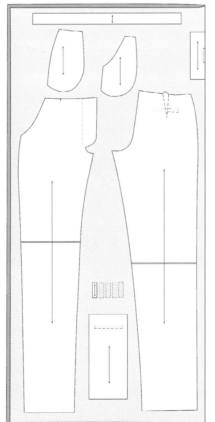

TOP TIPS FOR A GREAT FIT

Using fabric similar to the final garment, make a few toiles to get the adjustments right.

Get a buddy to help with fitting adjustments, especially on the back of the trousers.

Compare your pattern to a pair of trousers you already have. Lay the pattern on top and you'll be able to see any differences.

Practise making a fly zipper as it can be tricky at first.

A few quick tacking (basting) stitches will hold the trousers in place so you can try them on as you go before you stitch them together.

Remember to always trace off the pattern and work from the trace copy so that you have the original pattern intact.

FABRIC QUANTITIES

These quantities include enough fabric for facings.

SIZE	115cm wide	140cm wide
1	173cm/68"	155cm/61"
2	173cm/68"	155cm/61"
3	173cm/68"	155cm/61"
4	177cm/69½"	158cm/62"
5	177cm/69½"	158cm/62"
6	177cm/69½"	158cm/62"

MAKE THE TROUSERS

YOU WILL NEED

The trousers pattern pieces ⬦ Pattern paper ⬦ Paper scissors ⬦ Sticky tape ⬦ Tools for transferring marks ⬦ Fabric shears ⬦ Pins ⬦ Chosen fabric ⬦ Matching thread ⬦ 0.25m fusible interfacing, weight to suit fabric ⬦ 12/14cm zipper with metal teeth

PREPARE

1 Select the trouser pattern pieces. Trace the size you want to make onto pattern paper and cut out, keeping the original pattern intact.

2 Fold the fabric right sides together, as shown on the fabric layout diagram (see page 127). Place the paper patterns onto the fabric, aligning the grainlines.

3 Pin and cut out the fabric pieces. Before taking the pattern pieces off the fabric, be sure to transfer all the notches and other markings (see page 17).

4 Cut the pieces you require from the interfacing and stay stitch around the top of all four trouser pieces and the pocket linings.

INSERT THE FLY ZIPPER

5 Follow the instructions on page 50 to insert the fly zipper. **(A)**

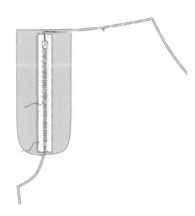

(A)

(B)

INSERT THE DIAGONAL POCKETS

6 Pin the pocket linings to the trouser fronts, right sides together, matching up the curved edges and side seams. Sew from the waist to the side seam. Trim the seam allowance and cut notches to reduce bulk. See page 62 for full pocket instructions and illustrations **(B)**

7 Work steps 11–16 for both pockets. Pull the pocket lining away from the trouser front, press the seam allowance towards lining and understitch in place.

8 Turn the lining back to the trouser front, wrong sides together. Press.

9 Working from the wrong side of the trouser front, place the pocket yoke on the pocket lining right sides together. Match the notches around the bottom curved edge and pin. Sew the pocket pieces together from the fly seam around the curve to the side seam.

10 Finish or bind the curved raw edge.

11 Working from the wrong side of the trouser front, pin the pocket yoke to the trouser front, making sure the pocket opening is flat underneath and none of the understitching is showing on the right side. Sew along the waist to the fly seam.

12 Still on the wrong side, sew the pocket to the side seam from the ridge of the pocket opening to the bottom of the pocket. Press.

SEW THE DARTS

13 Work steps 13–17 on each trouser back. Pin the right sides of the dart together at the waistline, matching up your tailor tacks or markings. Hold the dart so that the rest of the fabric falls away, making it easier to work with.

14 Secure the fold with pins at both ends. Using a ruler, draw a straight guideline for the dart from the cutting line to the dart point.

15 Using matching thread and straight stitch, sew the dart from the cutting line, along your guideline, to the point of the dart. Sew off the fabric.

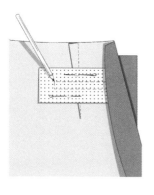
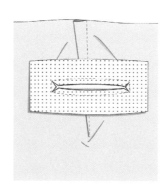
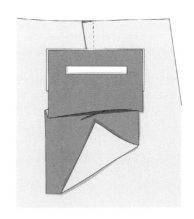

(C)

16 Cut the excess threads long so that you can tie them into a knot. This secures the stitching and gives you a nice sharp point.

17 Press your stitch line, then press the folded fabric in the dart towards the side seams.

SEW THE SINGLE WELT POCKETS

18 Follow the instructions on page 63 to sew the single welt pockets. **(C)**

PREPARE THE WAISTBAND AND BELT LOOPS

19 Prepare your belt loops. Fold the strip of fabric for the belt loops in half lengthways, wrong sides together. Press. Open out and fold the raw edges in to meet the fold line. Press again. Topstitch together down the open edge. You can topstitch down the folded edge for aesthetics if you wish. **(D)**

20 Fuse interfacing to the two pieces of fabric for the waistband.

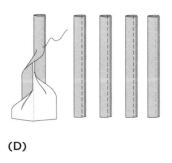

(D)

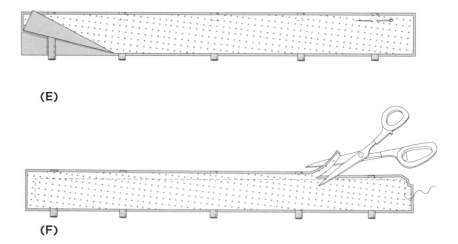

(E)

(F)

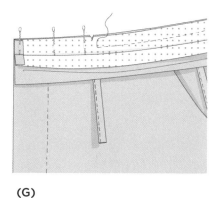

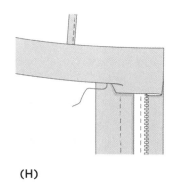

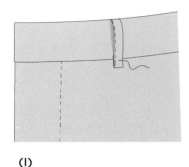

(G) (H) (I)

21 Decide where to position your belt loops. We used five belt loops for our make, placing one each mid-front, one at each side seam and one at the back by the back trouser seam. These points marry up with the notches on your waistband pattern.

22 Sandwich the belt loops inbetween the two waistband pieces inbetween the notches. Pin and tack (baste) the belt loops in position. **(E, page 130)**

23 Pin and sew the waistband together. Start at the narrow edge, 1.5cm from the cut edge and sew to the corner. Pivot then sew along the long edge of the waistband, over the belt loops. Continue to the other corner, pivot and finish 1.5cm from the cut edge. Trim away the excess seam allowance, layer and press to one side. **(F, page 130)**

24 Turn the waistband right side out and poke out the corners. Press.

ASSEMBLING THE TROUSERS

25 Pin the trouser front and back pieces right sides together. Sew the side seams, press, and finish the raw edges.

26 Carefully match up the centre back seam and the remaining part of the centre front seam. Pin in place and sew from the hem all the way

around the inside leg to the other hem. Press and finish the raw edges.

27 Turning the trousers right side out, pin the bottom layer of the waistband around the trouser waistline right sides together, matching the notches and making sure the seams align perfectly with the edge of the fly. **(G)**

28 Sew together and press. Trim and layer the seam allowance to minimise bulk all the way around (see page 60). Turn the waistband right sides out, making sure the top front corners are neat and square. Press.

29 Working on the inside of the trousers, fold the finished edge of the waistband under and slip stitch the fold in place along the waist seamline. Alternatively, work from the right side and topstitch through all the layers, as close as possible to the seamline to finish attaching the waistband, being careful not to catch the belt loops. Press. **(H)**. On the right side, fold the belt loop under and topstitch it in place **(I)** Add a trouser hook and eye to secure the top of the zip and waistband (see page 55).

30 Finish the trousers by turning up the hems. Turn under 1cm, then 1.5cm. Press, then topstitch on the machine.

Sister style
HIGH AND WIDE TROUSERS

We love a wide-leg trouser and this sister style is all about letting loose with a higher waist and wider leg. It also features a front fly fastening and diagonal front pockets.

Your fabric layout

This layout shows how the pattern pieces can be laid out on the fabric.

115cm wide fabric

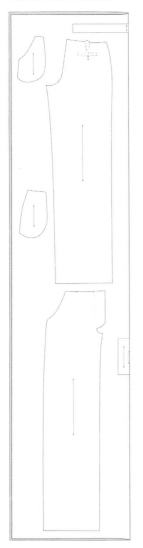

140cm wide fabric

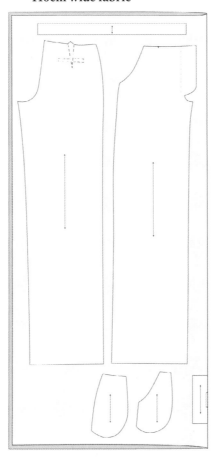

TOP TIP FOR A GOOD FIT

When you widen your trouser leg, adjust everything evenly so that the trouser leg doesn't twist. We only widened the legs, so the top of the trouser is still fairly fitted (see page 133).

FABRIC QUANTITIES

These quantities include enough fabric for facings.

SIZE	115cm wide	140cm wide
1	240cm/94½"	170cm/67"
2	240cm/94½"	170cm/67"
3	240cm/94½"	170cm/67"
4	240cm/94½"	230cm/90½"
5	240cm/94½"	230cm/90½"
6	240cm/94½"	230cm/90½"

YOU WILL NEED

The belt loop and welt pocket pattern pieces aren't needed for this make. The rest of the tools are the same as the main pattern.

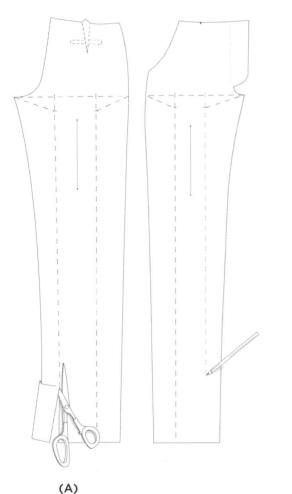

(A)

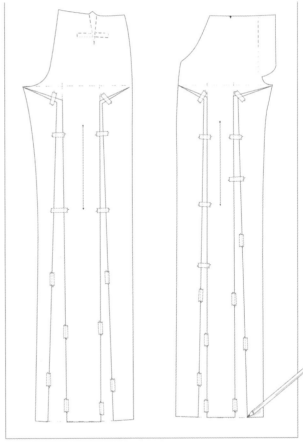

(B)

ADAPT THE WAIST

1 Decide where you want your trousers to sit. High-rise trousers usually sit on the waist.

2 Trace off your pattern pieces for the main trouser front and back. Lay them onto a new, slightly longer piece of paper. Pin in place.

3 Working with a ruler on the front trouser pattern, extend the side and front seams up by 2.5cm. Extend the dart, continuing the original dart lines so the dart is wider at the waistline.

4 Mark 2.5cm up from the original waistline at regular intervals. Connect the marks to draw a new waistline.

5 Repeat steps 3 and 4 on the back trouser pattern.

6 To adjust the waistline to fit your waist, divide your waist measurement by four. Use this quarter measurement to adjust the width of waistline by the same amount on both pattern pieces. You can make adjustments at the dart and/or the side seam, but remember not to include the seam allowance.

DIAGONAL POCKETS

If you adapted the waist you'll need to adapt the diagonal pocket pattern so that the patterns fit together.

CHECK THE CROTCH MEASUREMENT

7 Check your crotch measurement from your front waist, between your legs to your back waist.

8 Compare your crotch measurement with the pattern, by measuring around the centre front and back seams on the pattern pieces, not including seam allowances. If you need to make an adjustment, calculate the difference in the two measurements and halve that number. Cut a horizontal line across each pattern, between the waist and the crotch. Adjust the pattern by moving the cut edges apart or by overlapping them by the half measurement, as appropriate for your body.

9 Once you have adapted the pattern pieces, check all the measurements are correct and make a toile (see page 18) to decide on any final nips and tucks.

WIDEN THE LEGS

10 Cut out your new trouser pattern pieces and place them on a new piece of paper big enough to take wider legs.

11 On the trouser front pattern, measure across the hip line marking and make two marks to divide the line into three equal sections. Draw a vertical line from each mark to the hemline, keeping the lines parallel with the original seamlines. From the hip line mark 5cm down onto your newly drawn lines From this point draw diagonally up to the edge of the crotch to meet the hip line and the same on the other side. **(A, page 135)**

12 Cut along each new line and across the diagonal. You won't be cutting through anything just close enough to hinge. Temporarily pin or tape or use a fabric weight to keep the pattern in place, then fan each of the panels out to create 4cm gaps between the panels at the hem. Pin or tape them in place. **(B, page 135)**

13 Draw in the new hemline.

14 Repeat steps 11–13 for the trouser back pattern, keeping all the distances equal.

15 Cut the pattern pieces out, transferring any notches and markings.

ADJUST THE WAISTBAND

16 Trace off the pattern piece for the original trouser waistband. Measure the total waistline from the new trouser pattern pieces, remembering that you'll have two fronts and two backs, and excluding the seam allowances. Adjust the length of the waistband pattern to match. Transfer the markings from the original pattern, but adjusting the notches as necessary to match your new trouser back and front pattern pieces.

CUT OUT THE FABRIC

17 Place the paper patterns onto the fabric, aligning the grainlines.

18 Pin and cut out all the fabric pieces. Before taking the pattern pieces off the fabric, transfer all the markings (see page 17).

ADD POCKETS, FLY ZIPPER, DARTS AND WAISTBAND

19 Follow the instructions on page 62 to insert diagonal pockets.

20 Follow the instruction on page 50 to insert the fly zipper.

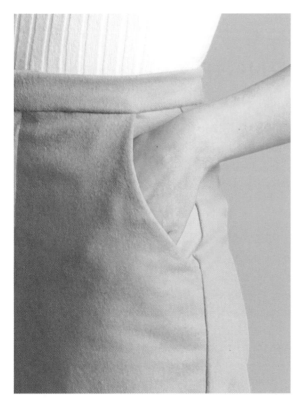

21 Refer to steps 17–21 from the main trousers to add the darts.

ATTACH THE WAISTBAND

22 Prepare the waistband as for the original trousers, but without the belt loops.

23 Sew up the trousers and attach the waistband, following steps 23–36 for the original trousers.

FINISH THE TROUSERS

24 Sew a hook and eye onto the waistband, following the instructions on page 55.

25 Finish the trousers by turning up the hems. Turn under 1cm, then 1.5cm. Press, then either hand stitch or machine stitch depending on your chosen fabric, following guidelines on page 44.

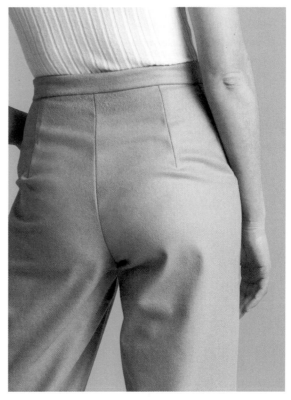

Make it your own
ADD A TURN-UP

A turn-up is a lovely addition to trousers. They're easy to add, but you need to extend the original pattern first. The instructions below are for a 4cm turn-up.

1 Before you cut the fabric and assemble the trousers, you will need to trace off the pattern pieces onto a longer piece of paper and extend the leg by 11cm (including 3cm for the hem allowance). Finish the bottom raw edge on each leg. Mark the finished length of the leg with a pin on the right side of the fabric 11cm from the bottom edge.

2 Place a second pin 4cm below the first, to mark the top of the turn-up then fold the bottom of the trouser leg up around the rest of the leg, right sides together. Fold the fabric so that the first pin is on the foldline. Pin the fold. **(A)**

3 Fold the bottom of the trouser leg down, wrong sides together, so that the second pin is on the new foldline. Pin the fold. **(B)** Tuck the hem allowance inside the trouser leg. Pin in place.

4 Check the depth is equal all the way round, then remove pins and press. Then re-pin the turn-up, placing the pins vertically and taking care not to pin through the front and back of the leg. **(C)**

5 Turn the trouser leg inside out. Remove the pins from the right side of the fabric and gently pull out the turn-up. Pin the hem allowance in place. Sew the finished edge in place or, alternatively, tuck the raw edge under and hem. Repeat for the other leg.

6 Turn the trousers right sides out and fold the turn-ups into place. They should cover the stitching. Press.

7 Line up the seamlines on the turn-ups and the trousers, and secure each turn-up to the trouser leg with small stitches on the side seams.

(A)

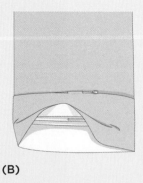

(B)

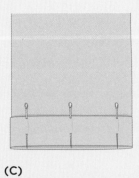

(C)

Add a crease

A purposeful crease down the front of trousers gives a crisp, sharp look. Creases work well on dressier trousers – and can make your legs look longer.

1 Before you start sewing, place the trouser front fabric pieces onto an ironing board. Fold each piece in half lengthways, wrong sides together. Set your iron as hot as the fabric can take and press the fold from the upper thigh to the hemline. Do not press to the raw edge as a crease can make it trickier to turn up the hem.

2 Double check you are happy with the position of the crease by placing the fabric against you. If it's not quite right, now is the time to change it. Press again.

3 Repeat on the other front piece, using the same measurements. Crease the back of the trousers in the same way, starting at crotch height so the crease doesn't go round your bottom.

KEEP CREASES IN PLACE

❖ Re-press the creases into your trousers every so often. The more you press, the longer the creases will last. Fibre memory!

❖ Use a pleat stick for very sharp, long lasting creases. Rub the stick along the crease on the wrong side of the fabric. Press the crease in place again on the right side.

❖ After pressing, roll a wooden rolling pin along the crease. According to this old wives' tale, this will help draw out the seam and set the creases in place!

NARROW THE LEGS

The basic trouser pattern in this book is for a straight leg. However, if you prefer a skinny option, you can make the legs narrower.

1 Trace off your pattern pieces for the main trouser front and back onto a new piece of paper.

2 On the new pattern pieces, bring the legs in equally on both sides of the front and back, making all adjustments from the hip line. Keep the new lines smooth and even, tapering towards the hemline. Don't forget that if you bring each line in by 1.25cm, the trouser leg will be 5cm narrower – a little adjustment goes a long way! You can always do the hinge technique (see page 135) to make the trouser wider but overlap instead of taking apart.

3 If the new trouser legs are tapered at the bottom, you need to taper the hem allowance in the opposite direction so that the finished hem doesn't pucker the trouser leg. Fold the pattern paper along the hemline and trace the side seam to give the hem allowance the correct shape.

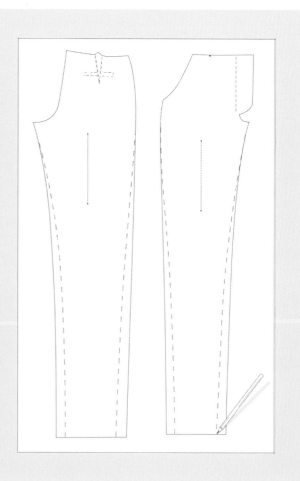

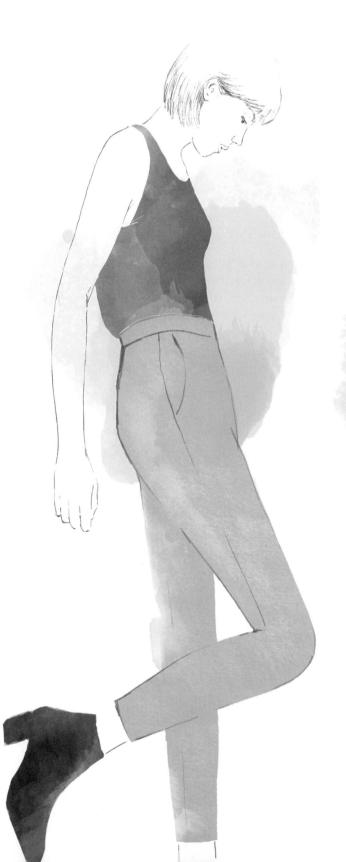

HOW SKINNY?

If you have a pair of skinny trousers that you love, use the shape of them to help create the contour you want on your new trousers. Trace around them onto the pattern pieces, remembering to add a seam allowance. If you're going for a super-skinny cut, check that you'll be able to get your foot through the bottom of the leg before cutting out your pattern. You can add a mini slit in the hem to help.

Make it your own
CULOTTES

Culottes have a loose voluminous shape, created by using a lot of fabric. Using lightweight fabric will give a soft billowy fullness

1 Trace off your pattern pieces for the basic trouser front and back onto a new piece of paper.

2 Mark a new hemline to fall to knee to mid-calf length, keeping it parallel to the original. Add a 2.5cm seam allowance. Make sure the front and back piece are the same length. Cut out the pattern pieces, including all markings.

3 Draw three equal lines vertically along the pattern. Don't cut into the arch or through a dart. It will interfere with your fly markings but you can redraw that in afterwards.

4 Cut up the lines to about 1.5cm from the waistline. Place these pieces on a new piece of paper and fan the pattern pieces out equally on both front and back. Decide how culottes-y you want them to be. If each gap is 7.5cm, that will be 22.5cm to the front and back making the total extra voluminosity 45cm – pretty swooshy!

5 Draw around the outside when happy with the shape; always check your measurements to make sure that are even on both sides – and cut out again – remember all markings. If you haven't changed the waist or rise of the pattern it should all fit together beautifully. Sew up as per instructions as detailed in the main project on page 128.

5

THE BLOUSE

A blouse makes the perfect companion to all the other garments. Its personality comes to life depending on the fabric and the cut you choose. It can be a quiet, chic, understated piece or make a dramatic entrance in a bold print or distinctive colour. Formal or relaxed, graceful or cute, a blouse can shift your mood too. The cuff detail on our design adds a dash of formality and the mandarin collar enhances the clean lines. Make it from a lightweight fabric and it'll have an inherent ethereal quality. Choose a mid-weight fabric and it'll have a more polished finish. The sister style is more relaxed, perfectly teamed with informal bell-shaped sleeves.

Crepe de chine

Features of the blouse

Monochrome print

Cotton lawn

Swiss knot

The blouse

Sister style: the holiday blouse

MAIN STYLE
The main blouse is fitted with front-fastening buttons. It features:
- a low mandarin collar
- full-length sleeves with cuffs
- an arched hem.

SISTER STYLE
The holiday blouse is a relaxed fit with an open v-collar.
It features:
- bell sleeves
- an elastic hem at the cuff
- a bias-bound neckline.

SUGGESTED FABRICS
This blouse works well in lightweight cotton, chiffon and linen. You can choose a bold print or a contrasting fabric to detail the button front, placket or collar. We made the main blouse using polyester crepe de chine and the sister blouse in cotton lawn with swiss knot.

Your pattern

The blouse has seven pattern pieces.

YOU WILL NEED TO CUT:

 2 FRONTS
 1 BACK ON THE FOLD
 4 BUTTON BANDS
 + 2 FROM INTERFACING
 2 COLLARS
 + 2 FROM INTERFACING
 2 SLEEVES
 2 CUFFS
 + 2 FROM INTERFACING
 2 PLACKETS
 + 2 PLACKET STRIPS
    FROM INTERFACING

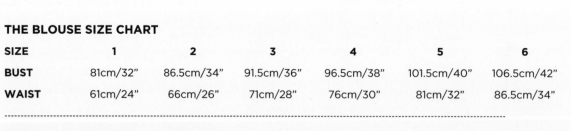

Button bands

Sleeve

Back

Front

Cuffs

Placket

Collar

Before you start

Take your measurements (see page 12) and then,
if necessary, grade the pattern if you are between
sizes (see page 16). We recommend making a toile
before making the final garment (see page 18).

THE BLOUSE SIZE CHART

SIZE	1	2	3	4	5	6
BUST	81cm/32"	86.5cm/34"	91.5cm/36"	96.5cm/38"	101.5cm/40"	106.5cm/42"
WAIST	61cm/24"	66cm/26"	71cm/28"	76cm/30"	81cm/32"	86.5cm/34"

FINISHED GARMENT MEASUREMENTS

The ease of the blouse around the bust is 12cm/4¾" and 29cm/11½" around the waist

SIZE	1	2	3	4	5	6
BUST	93cm/36¾"	98.5cm/38¾"	103.5cm/40¾"	108.5cm/42¾"	113.5cm/44¾"	118.5cm/46¾"
WAIST	90cm/35½"	95cm/37½"	100cm/39½"	105cm/41½"	110cm/43½"	115.5cm/45½"

Your fabric layout

This layout shows how the pattern pieces can be laid out on the fabric.

115cm wide fabric

140cm wide fabric

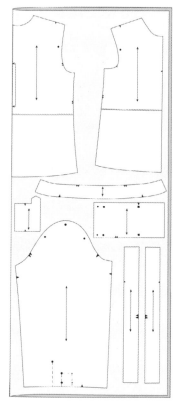
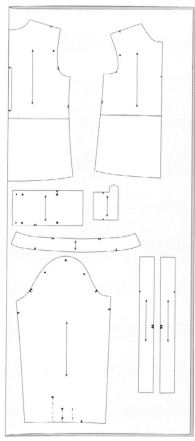

Remember to always trace off the pattern and work from the trace copy so that you have the original pattern intact.

- - - - - - - - - - - - - -

TOP TIP FOR SLIPPERY FABRICS

Place a sheet of calico or similar on your cutting table. This will stop the fabric from slipping – be careful not to cut through it, though!

FABRIC QUANTITIES

These quantities include enough fabric for facings.

SIZE	115cm wide	140cm wide
1	154cm/60½"	159cm/62½"
2	154cm/60½"	159cm/62½"
3	154cm/60½"	159cm/62½"
4	159cm/62½"	164cm/64½"
5	159cm/62½"	164cm/64½"
6	159cm/62½"	164cm/64½"

MAKE THE BLOUSE

YOU WILL NEED

The blouse pattern pieces ❁ Pattern paper ❁ Paper scissors ❁ Sticky tape ❁ Fabric scissors
❁ Tools for transferring marks ❁ Pins ❁ Chosen fabric ❁ Thread to match fabric
❁ 0.5m of lightweight fusible interfacing ❁ Fine, sharp sewing machine needle
❁ Twin needle (optional) ❁ 10 x 1.25cm buttons

PREPARE

1 Select the blouse pattern pieces. Trace the size you want to make onto pattern paper and cut out, keeping the original pattern intact.

2 Fold the fabric right sides together, as shown on the fabric layout diagram (see page 149). Place the pattern pieces onto the fabric, aligning the grainlines and making sure the edge marked 'FOLD' is on a fold of the fabric. Pin and cut out your fabric. Before taking the pattern pieces off the fabric, transfer all the notches and other markings (see page 17).

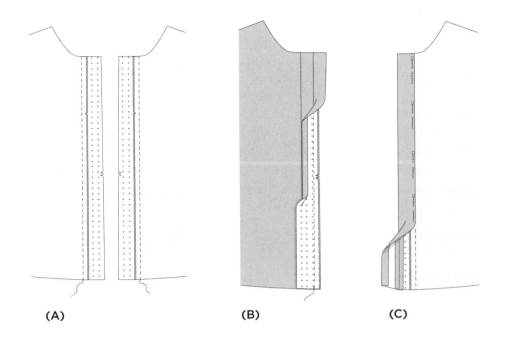

(A)   (B)   (C)

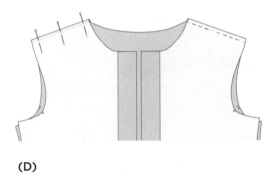

(D)

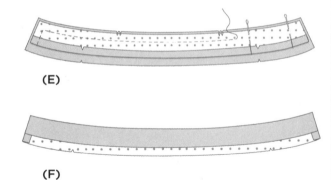

(E)

(F)

3 Cut the pieces you require from the interfacing. As with all our pieces we recommend making a toile. Stay-stitch the blouse neck.

ATTACH THE BUTTON BAND

4 Fuse interfacing to two of the button band/front pieces. Follow steps 5–9 to attach each button band.

5 Place one interfaced button band/front to a blouse bodice front, right sides together and matching the notches. Pin and sew in place. Press the seam allowance towards the button band. Trim the seam allowance. **(A)**

6 With the attached button band extended, pin a second button band piece to it to make a facing, right sides together and matching the double notches. Sew in place down the front seam.

7 Fold over the single notched edge on the facing by 1.5cm so that the fold sits neatly on the seamline on the button band. Press. **(B)**

8 Working on the wrong side of the blouse front, press the seam allowance towards each other and fold the button band facing over so that the folded edge sits slightly over the original stitch line. Press.

9 Pin, then tack (baste) this fold in place. It will be topstitched later. **(C)**

ASSEMBLE THE BLOUSE

10 Pin the blouse fronts to the blouse back at the shoulder seams and side seams. Pin them together wrong sides together if you want to make French seams (see page 40), which will enclose the raw edges neatly. If you wish to have straight stitched seams instead, sew the fabric right sides together, press, and finish the edges.

11 To sew French seams, follow the instructions on page 40. Having sewn the first line of stitching 5mm from the raw edge, sew the final line of stitching 1cm from the new folded edge. Press. **(D)**

ATTACH THE COLLAR

12 Staystitch around the blouse neckline and fuse the interfacing to one collar piece.

13 Turn over the single notched end on the interfaced collar piece by 1.5cm and press.

14 Pin both collar pieces right sides together, matching up the double notches. Sew the pieces together across each short end, securing the folded edge at those points, and along the top of the collar. Press, and trim the corners. **(E, page 151)**

15 Turn the collar right sides out. **(F, page 151)**

16 Pin the collar to the blouse, matching the raw edges. Firstly tack the collar in place, making sure not to catch the folded edge or the rest of the blouse. This helps to ensure the collar matches perfectly at the front of the blouse. Sew. Trim the seam allowance and press. **(G)**

17 Fold the collar facing over the raw edges. Pin, then topstitch or slipstitch it in place (see pages 39 and 36). **(H)**

ATTACH PLACKETS TO THE SLEEVES

18 Check you have transferred all the markings from the sleeve pattern to the fabric, including the slash line.

19 You need one placket piece and one smaller piece of interfacing for each sleeve. Make sure the slash line and sewing guidelines are also marked on the placket pieces.

20 Fuse the interfacing onto each placket, centrally along the long, pointed section. Then follow steps 20–29 to attach a placket to each sleeve **(I)**

21 Working on the wrong side, turn over the long raw edge by 6mm so it sits over the interfacing. Press. Repeat, to fold the opposite raw edge and then the edges on the point at the top of the placket. **(J)**

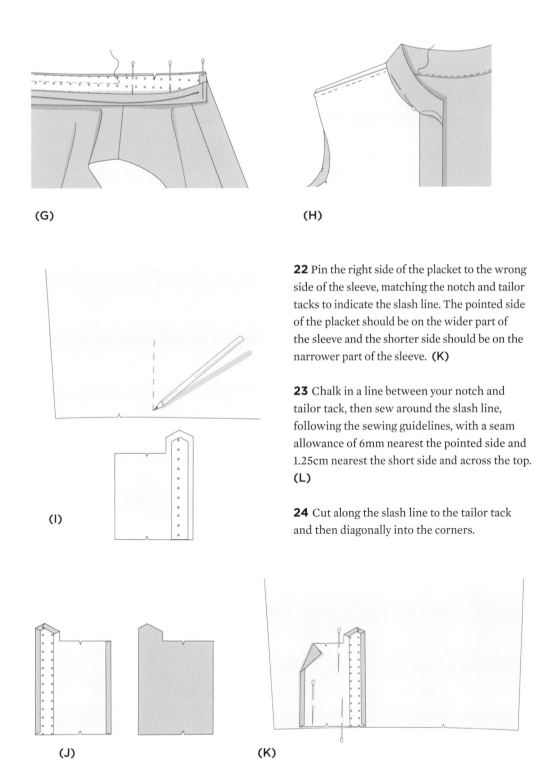

(G)

(H)

(I)

(J)

(K)

22 Pin the right side of the placket to the wrong side of the sleeve, matching the notch and tailor tacks to indicate the slash line. The pointed side of the placket should be on the wider part of the sleeve and the shorter side should be on the narrower part of the sleeve. **(K)**

23 Chalk in a line between your notch and tailor tack, then sew around the slash line, following the sewing guidelines, with a seam allowance of 6mm nearest the pointed side and 1.25cm nearest the short side and across the top. **(L)**

24 Cut along the slash line to the tailor tack and then diagonally into the corners.

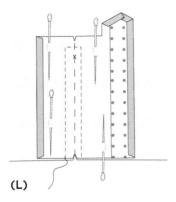

(L)

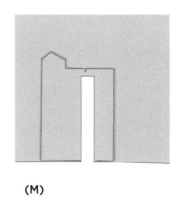

(M)

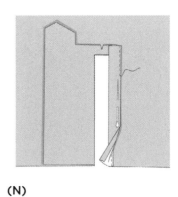

(N)

25 Turn the sleeve over and pull the placket through to the right side. Press the seams and the turnings flat. **(M)**

26 Working on the shorter side of the placket, fold the placket over the seam allowance so it sits slightly over the initial stitch line. Sew in place near the fold. **(N)**

27 Working on the pointed side of the placket, fold the placket over the seam allowance so that the folded edge just covers the initial stitch line.

28 Manoeuvre the placket so it fits neatly on the sleeve, covering the shorter side. Pin it in place, making sure the raw edges at the point are still turned under. On the front of the placket you will feel a ridge about 2.5cm from the point, place a horizontal pin where you feel this **(O)**.

29 Topstitch the placket in place, sewing across where the horizontal pin is, around the point, and down the other side that is already secured. Don't stitch down the open side. Sew slowly, pushing under any raw edges with a pin. Press. **(P)**

ATTACH THE CUFFS

30 Pin a small pleat on each sleeve, matching the notches. Baste in place, then follow steps 31–34 to attach a cuff to each sleeve. **(Q)**

31 Sew the underarm seam on the sleeve, matching the notches, with either a French or a straight stitched seam.

32 Turning to the cuff fabric, iron on the interfacing onto both pieces. Fold over the long edge with the twin notches by 1cm. Press.

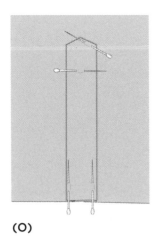

(O)

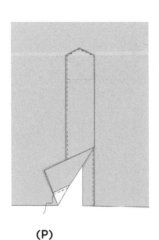

(P)

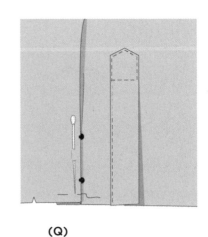

(Q)

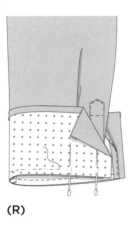
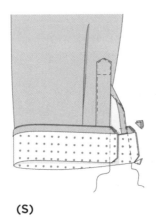
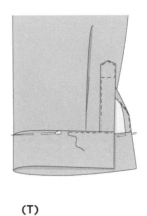

(R)   (S)   (T)

33 Pin, then sew the single notched unfolded edge to the bottom edge of the sleeve, right sides together and matching the notch with the underarm seam and each end of the cuff with the openings on the sleeve. Open out the cuff and press **(R)**. Then fold it back on itself, right sides together, so that the folded edges sit on top of each other. Sew across the ends. Trim the seam allowances. **(S)**

34 Turn the cuffs through to the right side and poke the corners out so they are nice and sharp. Press. Pin the folded edges in place, making sure the cuff is the same depth from one end to the other. Topstitch along the folded edge, making sure you catch the bottom layer, or slipstitch if you prefer. Topstitch along the bottom fold for added detail if you wish. **(T)**

INSERT THE SLEEVES

35 First, make sure you match each sleeve with the correct armhole! The plackets should face the back of the blouse. Then follow steps 36–40 to insert a sleeve into each armhole.

36 Sew two parallel lines of tacking in the seam allowance, this can be done by hand or on the machine around the sleeve head from one notch to the other. **(U)**

37 With the sleeve right side out, pin the side seam of the blouse to the seam on the sleeve, right sides together. Continue pinning the pieces together around the armhole seam, up to the notches. Pin the centre of the sleeve head to the shoulder seam, right sides together.

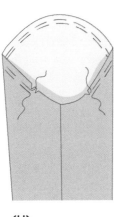
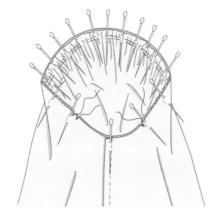

(U)   (V)   (W)

38 Gently pull the loose ends of the two threads so that the sleeve head gathers. Ease the sleeve head around the armhole and pin. Make sure the gathers are evenly distributed and use lots of pins. **(V, page 155)**

39 Tack (baste) the sleeve in place. Turn right sides out and check that the sleeve head sits well in the armhole without any puckers in the wrong place. Sew the sleeve in.

40 Press the seam allowance and the crown of the sleeve to iron out any small creases. Finish the raw edges.

FINISH THE BLOUSE
41 Open out the button band facings, ready to hem the blouse. Turn under 1.25cm along the bottom edge of the blouse. Press, then turn another 1.25cm press and pin. **(W, page 155)**

42 Fold the button band facings over the top of the hem, making sure the leading corners and square and that the facings don't sit below the hem. Make sure the button front meets evenly. Pin.

43 Topstitch the hem in place. If you would like a parallel stitch to finish the hem, you will need to use a twin needle.

44 Working from the right side, topstitch the button band, also securing the facing in place.

45 Decide if you want vertical or horizontal buttonholes, and where they should be positioned. We used six buttons for the front with 1.25cm diameter. Mark the positions for the buttonholes with pins on the right-hand button band (right, as you wear the blouse), and two buttonholes on the overlapping end of the cuff. Make sure they are centred on the button band and cuff.

46 Check the diameter of your buttons and set up your machine to do buttonholes. Follow the manufacturer's instructions to sew the buttonholes.. The buttonhole needs to be slightly smaller than the button for a secure fit.

47 Open each buttonhole with a seam ripper in one swift movement. It's helpful to insert a pin across the top of the buttonhole so you don't rip too far.

48 Stitch the buttons in place on the other button band, using complimentary thread to the buttons (see page 56).

Sister style
THE HOLIDAY BLOUSE

This blouse is more relaxed and looser than the main pattern, with slightly bell-shaped gathered sleeves, which drape beautifully over elastic hems.

Your fabric layout

This layout shows how the pattern pieces can be laid out on the fabric.

115cm wide fabric

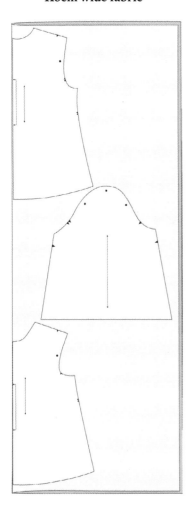

140cm wide fabric

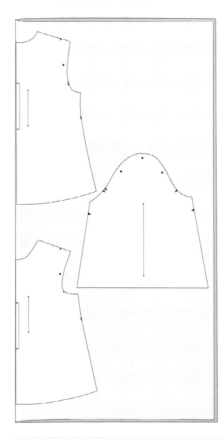

YOU WILL NEED

You will need the same materials as the main pattern, minus the button bands, collar, cuff, buttons and interfacing. In addition, you will need 127.5cm of bias binding and 60cm of 6mm-wide elastic.

TOP TIP FOR A GOOD FIT

We recommend making a toile before making the final garment (see page 18).

FABRIC QUANTITIES

These quantities include enough fabric for facings.

SIZE	115cm wide	140cm wide
1	160cm/63"	140cm/55"
2	160cm/63"	140cm/55"
3	160cm/63"	140cm/55"
4	160cm/63"	140cm/55"
5	160cm/63"	140cm/55"
6	160cm/63"	140cm/55"

ADAPT THE PATTERN

1 Trace off your pattern pieces for the main blouse front and back onto a larger piece of pattern paper.

2 Draw a new, lower neckline on both pattern pieces. We lowered ours by 5cm from the centre front, curving up to 2.5cm by the shoulders. and we lowered 2.5cm at the centre back, again curving to 2.5cm at the shoulders, making sure they match at the shoulder seams. Make small cuts in the paper to your new line, then fold the paper back and tape it down. This will give you more of an idea of how it will look and you can adjust.

3 Mark the length of the V-opening on the centre fold of the blouse front. We made ours 10cm long.

4 Extend the length of the blouse front and back by 4cm.

5 To create the looser fit, draw a line parallel to and 10cm from the centre front, from the hem to approximately 2.5cm under the bust point. Cut along this line and open out the shape by 5cm at the hem. The paper will pleat slightly, but just tape this down. Repeat for the blouse back. **(A)**

6 Now trace off your pattern piece for the basic blouse sleeve onto a larger piece of paper.

7 Mark the new sleeve length, including 1.5cm for the channel for elastic. We made our sleeve 4cm longer at the sleeve lengthening/shortening line.

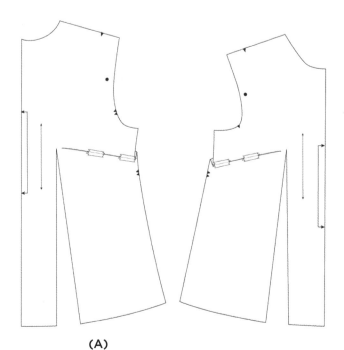

(A)

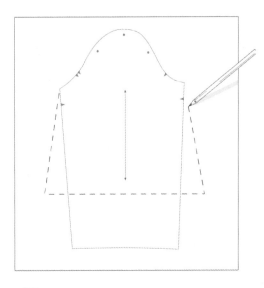

(B)

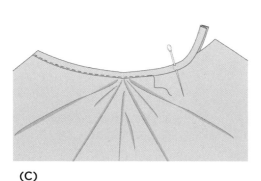

(C)

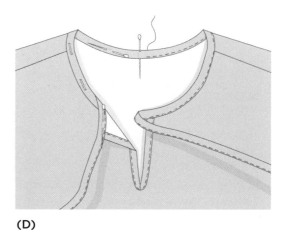

(D)

8 Make the pattern wider at the hemline by 7.5cm on each side for an exaggerated bell sleeve. Draw a line from each end of the new hemline to the top of the underarm seam. **(B)**

9 Trace off all the patterns onto new pattern paper, drawing smooth lines for the side seams and hems on the bodice pieces. Transfer all notches and markings.

10 Use the new pattern pieces to cut out the fabric, remembering to place the front and back on folds. Transfer all the notches and markings.

ASSEMBLE THE BLOUSE

11 Sew the shoulder and side seams as for the original blouse, matching the notches.

BIND THE FRONT OPENING AND NECK

12 Make enough bias binding to bind the opening on the blouse front (see page 43 for making bias binding). We used 4cm width bias binding stripes, making 1cm bias binding when folded.

13 Cut along the slash line on the blouse front.

14 You need about 25cm of bias binding for the V, including seam allowance. Opening up the

split, fold the binding over the cut fabric and pin in place. **(C)**

15 Topstitch all the layers together making sure you are catching the underneath layer. When you get to the split make sure you catch the base and it's not creeping out of the binding. The blouse will want to pucker and wrinkle underneath but go slowly and move the fabric to get a clean line.

16 Trim off the excess binding. Either leave the binding as a loose V-shape or, working on the wrong side, pinch the base into a V and sew diagonally across it.

17 Make enough bias binding to bind around the neckline. We used about 67.5cm for the neckline plus 30cm either side for the tie, equalling 127.5cm of bias binding. Attach the binding in the same way as the V but lining up the halfway mark of the binding with the centre back **(D)**. Alternatively, pin the right side of the bias binding to the right side of the neckline, lining up the raw edges. Sew along the fold, then press the seam allowance towards the binding.

18 Fold the binding over the seam allowance and either slip stitch or topstitch closed.

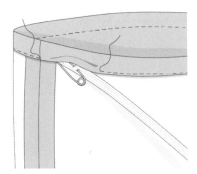

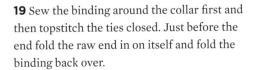

(E)

19 Sew the binding around the collar first and then topstitch the ties closed. Just before the end fold the raw end in on itself and fold the binding back over.

20 Stitch to the end making sure everything is tucked in. Press.

21 Add knots to tie up the ends or add tassels for added decoration.

INSERT THE SLEEVES

22 Pin and sew the side seams on each sleeve, matching the notches. Choose straight stitched seams or French seams as you wish. Press.

23 Aim to create a channel just a little wider than the width of your elastic. We used 5mm elastic. Turn up each hem by 5mm, then again by 1cm, to make a channel for the elastic. Press.

24 Sew each channel in place close to the top fold, leaving a short opening near the seam to insert the elastic.

25 Wrap the elastic once around the top of your arm and pull it to the desired tightness. We used 21.25cm. Mark this point and add 5mm more for sewing the elastic together. Cut two lengths the same.

26 Thread elastic into both sleeves in the same way. Attach a safety pin to each end of the elastic and thread one end through the channel. Gather the fabric on the elastic until you have both ends of elastic coming out of the same opening. **(E)**

27 Making sure the elastic hasn't twisted, overlap the two ends and sew them securely together.

28 Pull the cuff and the elastic will pop inside. Sew the opening closed.

29 Follow steps 36–40 for the main blouse to gather and insert the sleeves.

FINISH THE BLOUSE

30 Hem the blouse by turning up 1cm, then 1.5cm. Press and pin. Sew in place and press.

CHOOSE YOUR SLEEVES

Here are couple of additional sleeve alternatives for your blouse design to add to the selection on pages 120–121. The hemmed short sleeve has a more demure and understated design which is great for simple summer styling. The playful puff adds a perkier, more voluminous style that's easier to insert as you actively encourage the fabric to gather.

A SHORT SLEEVE WITH A DOUBLE HEM

1 Trace off your pattern for the main blouse sleeve onto another piece of paper.

2 Mark the new sleeve length, making sure the hemline is parallel to the original one. Short sleeves usually sit at mid-bicep, but it's up to you.

3 If you want the sleeve hem to be tighter or looser, adapt the sleeve pattern in a similar way to the sister style (see page 159).

4 Transfer all the notches and markings, including 2.5cm for a deeper hem.

5 Cut out the fabric and transfer all the markings. Sew, finish and press the underarm seams as usual. Turn up the hems and press. Then insert the sleeves into your blouse as for the main blouse.

ADD PUFF TO YOUR SLEEVES

1 Trace off your pattern for the main blouse sleeve onto a piece of paper.

2 Mark and cut the new length of the sleeve, including a hem allowance. We decided on a short puff sleeve, but the choice is yours.

3 You need to extend the width of the sleeve to create the puff, so draw three cut lines, one vertically down the centre line and the other two the same distance on each side of the first.

4 Cut along these lines from the sleeve head nearly to the hemline. **(A)**

5 Place the pattern on another piece of paper. Fan out the sleeve head so that the sections are evenly spaced. Redraw a new shape for the sleeve head, extending it above the old one, taking the shape of the outer pieces as your guide. **(B)**

6 Trace around the pattern, making the curves smooth.

7 Use your new pattern to cut out the fabric, transferring all notches and markings.

8 Sew, finish and press the underarm seams as usual. Turn up the hems and press.

9 Insert the sleeves into your blouse in a similar way as for the main blouse. When you are distributing the gathers, make sure there are gathers only between the notches. Inspect the gathers around the sleeve head while still basted. Then you can adjust them as necessary before sewing the sleeve on.

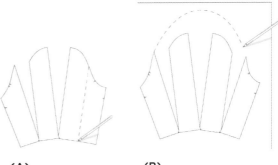

(A)   (B)

ADD A PUSSY BOW COLLAR

Different collars have a huge impact on a blouse and we have introduced a Peter Pan collar, a Chelsea collar and a pointed flat collar on page 118. Here we have opted for the very feminine pussy bow collar, which looks very effective in soft-drape, lightweight fabric. Avoid the 1980s corporate look by wearing your blouse with jeans or wide-leg trousers rather than a prim pencil skirt.

1 Decide where you want the bow to sit. It works well on a high neckline or on a deep V-shaped neckline. Adapt the pattern piece for the blouse front as necessary.

2 Measure around the whole neckline and add 60cm to this measurement to give the total length needed for the both ties.

3 Decide how wide you want the bow. Double this measurement and add 1.5cm for seam allowances.

4 Cut one strip of fabric according to your measurements in steps 2 and 3.

5 Fold the strip together, short ends together, and mark a notch at the centre point.

6 Temporarily pin the strip to the neckline and mark notches on the strip to match the shoulder seams and the centre fronts of the blouse.

7 Unpin the strip and refold it, long sides and right sides together.

8 Sew around the edges of the strip, with a 1.5cm seam allowance, from one notch marking the centre front on the blouse to the end of the strip and then across the short end. Repeat on the other end of the strip. Leave the centre section, which will be attached to the blouse, open. Layer the sewn seam allowances (see page 60).

9 Turn the strip right sides out. Poke out the corners so they look lovely and sharp. Turn under the seam allowances along the opening and press along the whole bow.

10 Open out the seam allowance and, matching notches and right sides together, pin one side of the bow to the blouse neckline. Trim the seam allowance or clip across it to help the neckline to curve. Press.

11 Turn the bow around and slipstitch or topstitch the remaining open edge close to the stitch line on the inside of the blouse. Press.

WANT A SHORTCUT?

If you're feeling confident, you can attach the bow to the blouse with one line of stitches. When you have sewn the bow strip together, leave an opening with seam allowances pressed inside. Pin the whole bow over the raw edge of the neckline. Topstitch it in place through all the layers, making sure you have enclosed all the raw edges.

CAPSULE COMBINATIONS

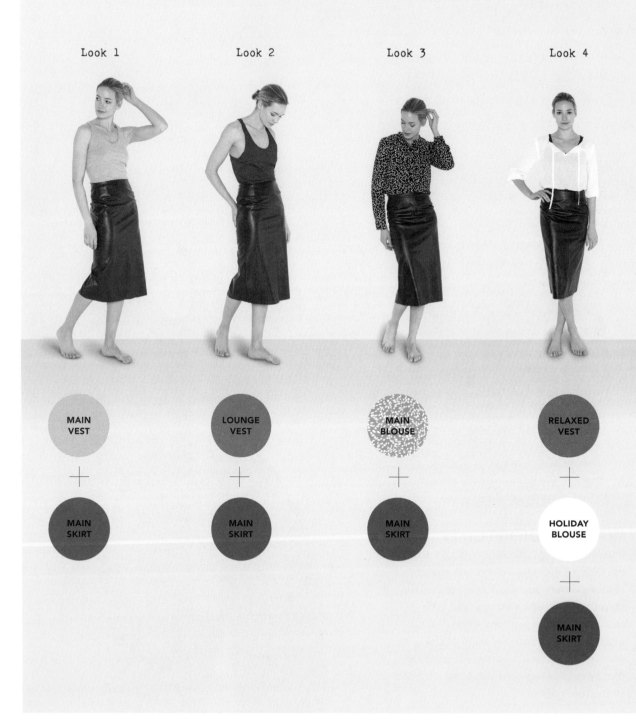

Look 1

Look 2

Look 3

Look 4

MAIN VEST

+

MAIN SKIRT

LOUNGE VEST

+

MAIN SKIRT

MAIN BLOUSE

+

MAIN SKIRT

RELAXED VEST

+

HOLIDAY BLOUSE

+

MAIN SKIRT

Look 5   Look 6   Look 7   Look 8

MAIN
VEST

RELAXED
VEST

MAIN
BLOUSE

LOUNGE
VEST

+

+

+

+

FLARED
MINI SKIRT

FLARED
MINI SKIRT

FLARED
MINI SKIRT

HOLIDAY
BLOUSE

+

FLARED
MINI SKIRT

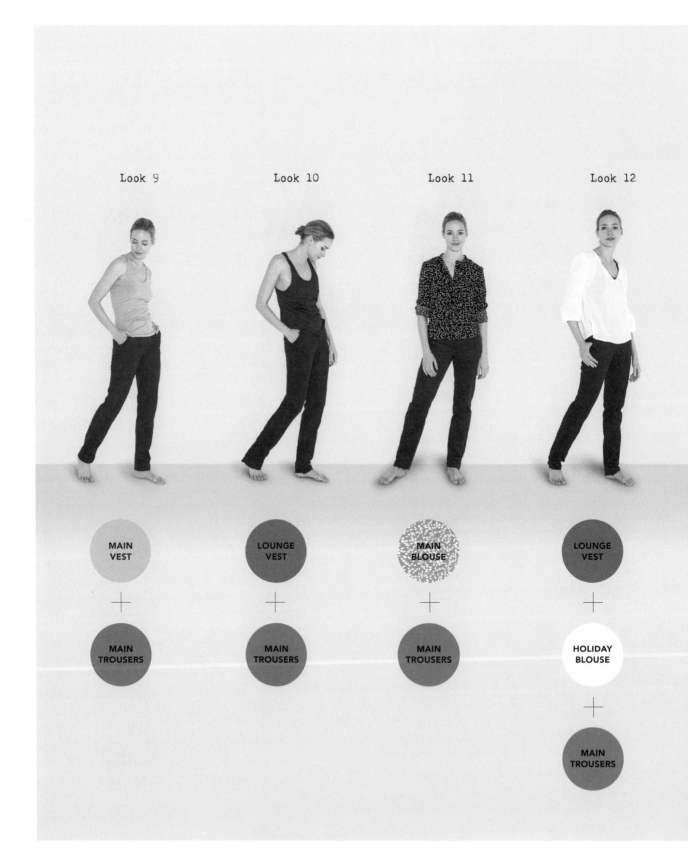

Look 9

Look 10

Look 11

Look 12

MAIN VEST

+

MAIN TROUSERS

LOUNGE VEST

+

MAIN TROUSERS

MAIN BLOUSE

+

MAIN TROUSERS

LOUNGE VEST

+

HOLIDAY BLOUSE

+

MAIN TROUSERS

Look 13   Look 14   Look 15

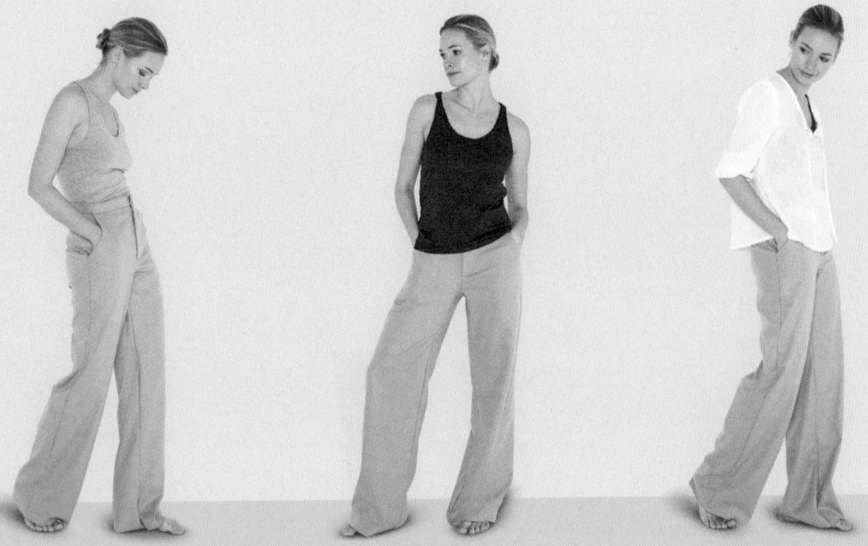

MAIN
VEST

LOUNGE
VEST

LOUNGE
VEST

+

+

+

WIDE
TROUSERS

WIDE
TROUSERS

HOLIDAY
BLOUSE

+

WIDE
TROUSERS

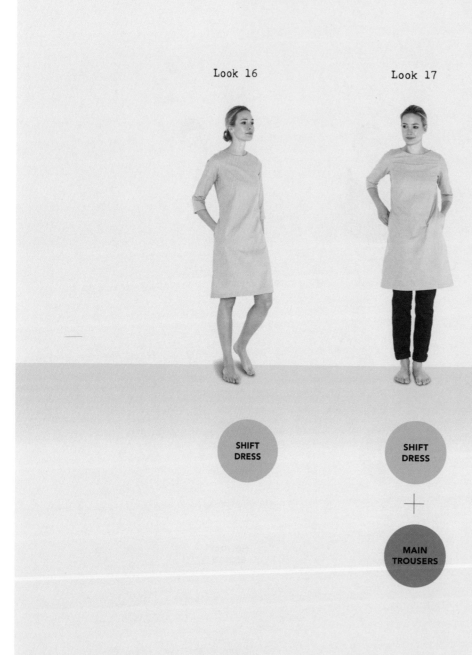

Look 16   Look 17

SHIFT
DRESS

SHIFT
DRESS

+

MAIN
TROUSERS

Look 18   Look 19   Look 20

TENT   TENT   TENT
DRESS   DRESS   DRESS

                 +   +

                 MAIN   MAIN
                 BLOUSE   BLOUSE

GLOSSARY

Bias binding – fabric cut on the bias in continuous strips and used on seam allowances and hems to create a neat finish. You can make your own or buy it readymade in an array of widths.

Blind hemming – when you turn up the edge of a garment and stitch so the stitches are hidden from the front of the garment.

Carbon copying – used for marking darts and pleats when transferring patterns

Back stitch (backtack) – this strong stitch can be used for sewing, mending seams and hemming.

Bust adjustment – adds or removes fullness to a garment around the bust area without losing the fit at the waist and shoulders.

Bust point – the point on the pattern where the point of the bust should fall.

Centre back – the middle of the back of a garment and pattern pieces.

Centre front – the middle of the front of a garment and pattern pieces.

Cutting lines – these show the same of each pattern piece.

Dart – folds sewn into fabric to manage the fullness of a garment to shape around the contours of the body usually found at the bust and waist.

Ease – the difference between the measurements of a finished garment compared with the actual body measurements.

Fabric layout – a diagram illustrating the best way to lay the pattern pieces onto the fabric.

Facing – layer of fabric on the inside of edges of a garment to finish the raw edge where a hem isn't possible or not sufficient. Usually found at necks, on armholes of sleeveless garments, on waists instead of a waistband and sometimes on hems.

Fold line – where you line up the pattern with a fold along the fabric.

Gathers (ruches) – excess fabric brought together with parallel rows of loose stitching.

Grading – the skill of changing a pattern to fit your own exact measurements.

Grain/Grainline – lengthways direction of a fabric, parallel to the selvedges. The grain of the fabric in the finished garment affects how it will hang and drape.

Half slip stitch – invisible stitch used for seams and hems.

Hem – a way to neaten the edge of a piece of fabric.

Herringbone stitch – almost invisible from the right side, this stitch is perfect for hand stitching hems.

Interfacing – fabric that is attached to the wrong side of your fabric to stiffen and strengthen areas of wear and tear or to help keep their shape. Most often used in waistbands, button stands, collars and cuffs.

Notches and snips – marks on the edge of patterns pieces to help match seams accurately.

Overlocker (serger) – a specialised type of sewing machine that stitches, cuts and finishes raw edges.

Pressing – different to ironing, which moves your iron repeatedly across fabric or a garment to remove creases, pressing uses your iron slowly in specific areas to flatten and smooth your sewing, e.g. seams, hems, darts to make your sewing look much neater and more professional.

Quick Unpick – a handy tool with a sharp pointed edge that unpicks any unwaanted stitches.

Raw edge – cut edge of fabric that should be neatened to prevent fraying through edge finishing.

Right side – the side of the fabric that ends up on the outside of the garment.

Rise – the distance from hip to waist: sit on a table and cross one leg over the other. Measure from the waist down to the table on the upper leg side. This is your rise measurement.

Seam – stitching that joins together pieces of fabric.

Seam allowance – the distance between the cut edge of the fabric piece and the seamline.

Seamline – position of the seam stitching along a piece of fabric.

Selvedge (selvage) – neat finished edges on fabrics that runs in the lengthwise direction along the grainline, useful in identifying the straight grain.

Slip stitch/ladder stitch – stitch used to sew two folds together – for instance on lining when you can't get to the seam allowance.

Stitch in the ditch – sewing along a seamline from the right side after the seam has been pressed open.

Straight stitch – universal machine setting, straight stitch is used for seams and topstitching.

Tacking (basting) – to check the fit of a garment by temporarily holding it together using large running stitches or to hold fabric in place to prevent slipping before permanent stitching.

Tailor's chalk – a piece of chalk used to mark fabric.

Toile (muslin) – a sample or practice garment to try out the fit of a pattern and make any necessary corrections before constructing the final garment.

Tracing off – to trace the original or graded pattern onto new pattern paper in order to keep the original pattern intact.

Trousers – US pants.

Understitch – machined straight stitch that helps seamlines sit neatly on the inside of a garment, most often used along facing seams.

Waistband – a separate piece of fabric used to finish the waist of trousers (pants) and skirts.

Wrong side – the side of the fabric that ends up on the inside of the garment.

RESOURCES

FABRIC

Fabrics Galore
52-54 Lavender Hill,
London SW11 5RH
fabricsgalore.co.uk
Our personal favourite.
Fabulous choice of fabrics
with the best printed
cottons

Borovicks Fabrics
16 Berwick St,
London W1F 0HP
borovickfabrics.com

The Cloth House
47 Berwick Street
London W1F 8SJ
clothhouse.com

Liberty London
Regent St, Carnaby,
London W1B 5AH
libertylondon.com

Barnett Lawson - Fitzrovia
16/17 Little Portland Street,
London W1W 8NE
bltrimmings.com
Great treasure trove
of trimmings

VV Rouleaux
102 Marylebone Lane,
London W1U 2QD
vvrouleaux.com
Gorgeous range of ribbons
and trimmings

The Button Queen
19 Marylebone Lane,
London W1U 2PR
thebuttonqueen.co.uk
Every button you can think of!

The Cloth Shop
290 Portabello Road,
London W10 5TE
theclothshop.net

MacCulloch & Wallis
25-26 Poland Street
London W1F 8Q
macculloch-wallis.co.uk

Jasons Fabrics
310–312 Edgware Road,
London W2 1DY
jasonsfabrics.com
Designer prints, French lace,
printed cottons.

Morplan
Stores in London West
End, Bristol, Glasgow,
Birmingham
morplan.com
All equipment, pattern paper,
scissors, dummies, books etc

Abakhan
Stores in Altrincham,
Birkenhead, Bolton, Chester,
Hanley, Stoke-on-Trent,
Liverpool, Manchester,
Mostyn North Wales,
Preston
abakhan.co.uk
One of the UK's leading
suppliers of fabrics, crafts
and haberdashery.

Fabric Land
Stores in Basingstoke,
Bournemouth, Brighton,
Bristol, Kingston London,
Portsmouth, Reading,
Salisbury, Southampton
fabricland.co.uk

Belle Fabrics
6-12 Elm Road, Leigh on Sea,
Essex SS9 1SN

Guthrie & Ghani
169 Alcester Road, Moseley
Birmingham, B13 8JR
guthrie-ghani.co.uk

Mandors Fabric Store
134 Renfrew Street, Glasgow
G3 6ST
mandors.co.uk

Edinburgh Fabrics
12-14 St Patrick Square,
Edinburgh EH8 9EZ
edinburghfabrics.co.uk

Til The Sun Goes Down
Original fabrics and clothing
inspired by the 1920s through
to the 1960s.
tilthesungoesdown.com

John Lewis Haberdashery
johnlewis.com

The Fabric Godmother
Independent fabric website
with gorgeous fabrics packed
with style.
fabricgodmother.co.uk

The Sewbox
Stylish sewing patterns,
beautiful fabrics, and
convenient all-in-one
pattern packs.
sewbox.co.uk

Patch Fabrics
An array of fabrics plus great
sewing kits and patterns.
patchfabrics.co.uk

We Love Fabric UK
Purveyors of fine
cotton fabrics.
welovefabric.co.uk

Jaycotts
Brilliant for dressmaking
patterns
jaycotts.co.uk

William Gee
Leading stockists of Spot &
Cross Paper, calico, elastics,
Fiskars Products, manilla
card, Coats Threads and
YKK Zips.
williamgee.co.uk

Minerva Crafts
One stop shop for everything
sewing, knitting and craft.
minervacrafts.com

The Sewing Directory
A fantastic spot not just for
suppliers but all things sewing
related including sewing
events and projects.
thesewingdirectory.co.uk

MACHINES
The Wimbledon Sewing Machine Company
craftysewer.com

US SUPPLIERS
Jo-Ann
joann.com

Michael's
michaels.com

Rifle Paper Co
riflepaperco.com

ACKNOWLEDGEMENTS

This book wouldn't have been possible without the brilliance of such talented people including:

– Tara O'Sullivan for her continual patience, kindness and razor sharp editing skills.

– Kyle Cathie and Judith Hannam for championing the original idea and allowing us the freedom to make the book we wanted to make.

– Paula Blanche and Robin Blair whose illustrations brought the intricate instructions in this book to life.

– Amanda Thomas for her beautiful photography assisted by Beata Stencel.

– Scott Purnell for his design and creative excellence and Amelia Pruen for her make up, styling and all round expertise on the shoots.

– The models – Alex, Danea and Anna Sophie who wore each garment so exquisitely.

– Paul Johnston of Fabrics Galore who so generously gifted us all the fabric for the garments in this book.

– Helen Barton and Deborah Shepherd from Janome, without their machines nothing would be stitched!

– Dawn O'Porter for her top tips and encouragements.

– Grade House for grading the patterns so clearly.

– And finally Bob Dog, for keeping our spirits up.

Arianna would personally like to thank:

– My wonderful husband Trev, for your unwavering support, love and encouragement and for never mentioning being covered in threads from dawn to dusk.

– My family – thank you Mum, Dad and my gorgeous sisters for your resolute faith and love and growing up in such a fun, colourful and creative home by the sea.

– My super bro-in-laws, littl'uns and my new Australian family.

– My dear friends for late night laughs and dealing with me being a hermit for the last year.

– My teachers at Sewing Sessions and the girls we have taught to sew. I am so grateful to be in an industry where I am constantly learning and being inspired.

Cathy would personally like to thank:

– My dearest family, especially my sister Saba who champions every endeavour I undertake. She's my biggest fan and I am hers.

– My precious friends Mano, Cathy and Hayley for their constant encouragement and support.

– And finally my Justin, for providing love, kindness and unending support and for allowing me to squirrel myself away month after month to complete this book.

An Hachette UK Company
www.hachette.co.uk

First published in Great Britain in 2017
This edition published in 2021 by Kyle Books, an imprint of
Octopus Publishing Group Limited
Carmelite House
50 Victoria Embankment
London EC4Y 0DZ
www.kylebooks.co.uk
www.octopusbooksusa.com

ISBN 978 0 85783 393 8

Distributed in the US by Hachette Book Group, 1290 Avenue of the Americas, 4th and 5th Floors,
New York, NY 10104

Distributed in Canada by Canadian Manda Group, 664 Annette St., Toronto, Ontario, Canada M6S 2C8

PROJECT EDITOR: Tara O'Sullivan
EDITORIAL ASSISTANT: Isabel Gonzalez-Prendergast
COPY EDITOR: Katherine Hemingway
DESIGNER: Cathy McKinnon
PHOTOGRAPHER: Amanda Thomas
FASHION ILLUSTRATOR: Paula Blanche
TECHNICAL ILLUSTRATOR: Robin Blair
HAIR AND MAKE-UP ARTIST: Amelia Pruen
PRODUCTION: Lisa Pinnell

A Cataloguing in Publication record for this title is available from the British Library.

COLOUR REPRODUCTION BY ALTA LONDON
PRINTED AND BOUND IN CHINA

10 9 8 7 6 5 4 3 2